To Father and Mother

SHAKESPEARE'S DRAMATIC STYLE

JOHN RUSSELL BROWN

Shakespeare's
Dramatic Style

ROMEO AND JULIET

AS YOU LIKE IT   JULIUS CAESAR

TWELFTH NIGHT   MACBETH

BARNES & NOBLE, Inc.
NEW YORK
PUBLISHERS & BOOKSELLERS SINCE 1873

© John Russell Brown 1971
First published 1971

ISBN 0 389 04064 9

First published in the United States 1971
by Barnes & Noble, Inc.

Printed in Great Britain

Contents

Preface

THIS book starts as a guide on 'How to read Shakespeare'. But it also raises major issues about our understanding of Shakespeare: how much should we read as if we were directors of productions, or actors, and how can we do this? to what extent did Shakespeare allow us to read ourselves and our own concerns into his plays? where and how did he allow for a variety of interpretations? where are the plays intentionally ambiguous? when are words important, when silence or gesture? how are the meanings of silence and gesture controlled? in what ways, and by what means, is Shakespeare a realistic writer? how can we recognize major dramatic crises, especially those which depend on the excitements of acting? how much was Shakespeare confined by the conditions of theatrical performance in his own day?

In fact, no one with a mind open to Shakespeare's dramatic style could write a simple book: the style is not simple. Once we start asking questions about the first impressions we have gained, whether from productions or from readings, we are caught up in one of the most fascinating, minutely worked and, in several senses of the word, *large* creative achievements that the world has known. We can seek simple responses among others, but we must always be prepared for complicated explanations. The writing of this book was a sustained adventure in understanding, and I hope, above all, that the record of my thoughts will encourage readers to undertake such investigation for themselves.

The five plays I have considered are among those most frequently performed and read. Four of them I have directed in England or the United States: *Romeo and Juliet* and *As You Like It* at the Playhouse, Cheltenham, *Macbeth* at the Everyman, Liverpool, and *Twelfth Night* at the Playhouse, Pittsburgh, and for Channel 13 TV, New York. I am greatly indebted to my casts for their contribution to my knowledge of these plays. *Julius Caesar* I have often seen in performance, notably at the Royal Shakespeare Theatre, Stratford-upon-Avon; I am especially indebted to the 1968 production there.

Texts have been quoted from *The Players' Shakespeare*, ed. J. H. Walter, by kind permission of the editor and the publishers, Heinemann Educational Books Ltd, London. I have occasionally simplified the stage-directions, reverting to the bare indications of the original editions.

JOHN RUSSELL BROWN

Churchill, Worcestershire

PART ONE

1 Introduction

MY AIM is to teach how to read Shakespeare's text creatively, to show by example how to explore, sift and possess a passage for oneself in something like its full theatrical life.

The literary qualities of a Shakespeare play are easily enough grasped, once they have been described, but not its theatrical energy and life; for this, the best way that I have found is to study comparatively short passages in great detail and in a theatrical context. I do not want to nail down 'meanings' or offer 'interpretations', but to consider what the words ask actors to do, and what the enacted drama may do for an audience in performance. By opening our minds to every discernible detail of short moments of a play in performance, we may meet with Shakespeare's dramatic imagination at work, with all the richness and subtlety of his involvement in a three-dimensional, almost living, image of life. In short, my book is an introduction to Shakespeare. But not because it is elementary or because it provides the basic facts and commonly accepted opinions: it tries to effect an introduction.

I would most like to teach a method, a means of careful, patient encounter which my readers can then follow, adapt and, no doubt, simplify for themselves. I have found that to talk about a play's significance or meaning is to recount one's own opinion or someone else's. Opinions are plentiful, and they can be well informed, up-to-date and, sometimes, imaginatively arousing. But there is no substitute for an open encounter on one's own account with what happens in a play. Without reaching all the time for significance or interpretations, we can remain open-minded before a play, choosing one moment and then another; we can turn it first this way and then that, observing, marking and trying to respond imaginatively to what is there, hidden within

3

the words printed on the page. There will be time enough to evaluate what we have found when the special effort required for this kind of introduction has been, for the time being, exhausted. The first and demanding step is to encounter the text of the play and all its manifold implications and suggestions, each for oneself.

Some method, some introductory procedures, are necessary. Otherwise we may get lost in those aspects that most easily catch our attention. I do not mean the aid of editorial annotation and glossaries; these cope with the obvious difficulties brought about by changes in the language, life and ideas of men. Of course we should pay attention to footnotes. The further and more persistent trouble is that the printed words are only clues to Shakespeare's plays, and we must learn to seek out, within them and beyond them, the full heard, seen and experienced image of life of which they are only one element – and sometimes not the most important.

How can we sit down and 'read' a play? It is at least as specialized an activity as reading a musical score so that we hear the music in our imagination; only words do not indicate time, pitch, and volume like musical notation. It is like imagining a landscape from 'reading' a map; or judging the personality and physical presence of some unknown writer of a letter. It is like trying to imagine a dramatic episode in real life, not by listening outside the closed door of a room you know as people you know are talking, but by reading a transcript of what was said, with little or no indication of the setting and no previous knowledge of the participants. But the task is not quite as hopeless as it might appear, for Shakespeare chose words that do reveal other elements of the situation, such as tone of voice and speed of delivery – if we know how to look for these clues to the physical and temporal drama.

Take a simple example: when we watch a play in performance certain words will stand out, force themselves upon our attention. However the production is staged and performed, some words in the performance of the play are as if they were in great capital letters; others are almost invisible: and yet on the printed page every letter is the same size, no word standing out from its fellows.

Or suddenly all attention in a theatre is focused upon a silent figure, perhaps walking off stage while others speak: for this on the printed page there is simply the one word '*Exit*', which cannot suggest the manner of leaving the stage nor the way in which the silent character has usurped attention when the printed page is full of the words of others. We must learn to read a text so that such theatrical facts are clear to us, in the theatre of our minds.

Of course it is helpful to see plays in performance. But this is no substitute for learning to see and hear them for ourselves. Firstly, while a play is in performance we must yield to its momentary excitements and cannot wait, even if we wished to, to make sure we have responded fully to what is happening, or to verify and extend our impressions. Secondly, every production is limited in its achievement: unsuitable stage or auditorium, too little rehearsal time, too much or too little money to be spent, some inadequate casting, and always the particular talents and individual ambitions of director, designer and actors – all this affects what we see and hear. Constant theatre-goers will be satisfied, because each new production has its own revelations, and so a complex understanding of a play can be built up over the years. But we cannot always see the plays we want to study in an appropriate number of varied and imaginative productions. If we are interested in Shakespeare on our own accounts, there is no other course but to learn to see and hear the plays for ourselves. In this way we will always imagine our own production; we shall learn from the productions of experienced actors and directors, but we shall also confront Shakespeare independently, so that his plays will seem to reflect our world and extend our own imaginations. We shall keep the plays in continuous rehearsal in our own minds.

I believe it is only after we have gained some knowledge of what the printed words imply in terms of performance, when we have a grasp of the dramatic style of a play, that the wider questions of criticism and scholarship are truly valuable. Then we are able to test the value of each opinion by our own response to the text, and be in a sure way to become responsible critics in our turn.

2 *The Evidence*

BEFORE considering how to realize the theatrical life implicit in the printed words of Shakespeare's plays, we must take time to ask how reliable those words are as evidence of Shakespeare's intentions. His plays are quite unlike those of a contemporary dramatist printed from typescripts prepared from their author's autograph copies, and corrected at proof stage by the author himself.

Shakespeare seems to have taken little or no interest in the publication of his plays. Many were printed only after his death and, as far as we know, he proof-read none of the earlier publications, as did some of the more literary dramatists of his time. Some of the early editions were printed from very ill-prepared manuscripts, or from two different copies simultaneously. *Romeo and Juliet*, the first play considered in this book, is an interesting example. The earliest edition appeared in 1597 and is called, today, the 'Bad Quarto': 'Quarto' because, in common with most other plays printed in a volume of its own, it was printed on sheets of paper each folded twice to form four leaves; and 'Bad' because it is obviously far from the text Shakespeare wrote or the Chamberlain's Men performed. This was a 'pirated text': probably some actors had copied down what they could remember of the play and were paid a pound or two for their labour by a publisher eager to issue a version of a popular success. It has many omissions; it is often ungrammatical, unmetrical and confused; not a few lines make nonsense and more are trite or clumsy. The most interesting feature is perhaps some stage directions which read like eye-witness reports of performance: '*They whisper in his ear*'; '*Enter Juliet somewhat fast, and embraceth Romeo*'; and so on. Two years later the 'Good Quarto' appeared from a different publisher. For the most part this seems to have been set from one of Shakespeare's own manuscripts, with stage-directions that vary the names of characters and with some passages repeated in amended versions, so that the printed text gives the author's first thoughts and his developed version side by side. But in the printing-house there was also a copy of the Bad Quarto, and sometimes, perhaps when Shakespeare's handwriting was particularly difficult to read, the compositor consulted this pirated text and reproduced its reading. The most consistent use of the Bad Quarto was between I. ii. 52 and I. iii. 34. These two editions – each imperfect – together with the Folio edition of 1623 that was printed from a second printing of the Good Quarto, are the only evidence we have of Shakespeare's play and so, in choosing passages for close examination and exploration, we should make sure that the text is wholly from the Good Quarto and without hints of repetition or incomplete composition.

The other plays considered in this volume have less complicated textual histories, each first appearing in the collected Folio edition of Shakespeare's plays of 1623. *As You Like It* and *Twelfth Night* were printed from the prompt-book used by the King's Men, the company in which Shakespeare himself was an active proprietor, or, possibly, from a transcript made from this source. The other two plays are also dependent on theatrical manuscripts, *Julius Caesar* being printed from a transcript of a prompt-book that was quite possibly in Shakespeare's own handwriting, and *Macbeth*, less fortunately, from a version prepared for court performance and possibly altered by cuts and additions for this occasion. For each play of Shakespeare's it is necessary to find out about its textual authority and bear this in mind while trying to discover the full implications of its words.

When the manuscript reached the printing-house all was not straightforward. Here more corruptions inevitably ensued, especially in spelling, elision, use of italics and capitals, verse-lining, arrangement of stage-directions and so forth. In a play, these can be details of large consequence. Consider the one-word speech: 'No!' Perhaps it should read 'No?', or, more simply, 'No.' It might be a line by itself, breaking the flow of iambic pentameters, or possibly it should be fitted in at the end or beginning of another verse-line whose slight irregularity could contain this one stress without disturbing the underlying metrical pattern. For a text written to be spoken these details are of great importance.

Read the following speech aloud, pausing appropriately at each mark of punctuation:

> O, by your leave, I pray you,
> I bade you never speak again of him:
> But, would you undertake another suit,
> I had rather hear you to solicit that
> Than music from the spheres.

Then read this following version, also aloud and pausing according to the weight of the punctuation:

> O by your leave I pray you.
> I bade you never speak again of him;
> But would you undertake another suit
> I had rather hear you, to solicit that,
> Than Music from the spheres.

The first is from III. i of *Twelfth Night* as it appears in the Globe Shakespeare, one of the most commonly used texts; the second is from the Folio of 1623; and the second to my ear gives an eagerness and sharpness of mind that are hidden by the sensible, decorous punctuation of the modern editor's version. The speaker is Olivia, a young girl in love for the first time.

Or consider Brutus soliloquizing in his orchard:

> He would be crown'd:
> How that might change his nature, there's the question.
> It is the bright day that brings forth the adder;
> And that craves wary walking. Crown him? – that: –
> And then, I grant, we put a sting in him,
> That at his will he may do danger with.
> The abuse of greatness is, when it disjoins
> Remorse from power: and, to speak truth of Caesar,
> I have not known when his affections sway'd
> More than his reason.

Read that version aloud first, and then this:

> He would be crown'd:
> How that might change his nature, there's the question?
> It is the bright day, that brings forth the Adder,
> And that craves wary walking: Crown him that,
> And then I grant we put a Sting in him,
> That at his will he may do danger with.
> Th'abuse of Greatness, is, when it dis-joins
> Remorse from Power: And to speak truth of *Caesar*,
> I have not known, when his Affections sway'd
> More than his Reason.

Some of this is not easy to read: but clearly it has different emphases, especially around the crucial 'question' and 'Crown him that'. Perhaps the capital letters suggest special emphasis, as the 'M' for 'Music' in the last line of the Folio version of Olivia's speech – but then it is surprising that 'question' is not so emphasized, unless Brutus reaches the point almost in spite of himself. . . . It is a subtle business to translate printed punctuation into speech.

One more example, from *Macbeth*, shows how much a single comma can accomplish:

> When the hurly-burly's done,
> When the battle's lost, and won.

Remove the Folio's punctuation after 'lost', as almost every modern editor has done, and the antithesis with 'won' is not so assertive or threatening.

Unfortunately we cannot simply prefer the punctuation of the earliest editions. Some of these, as we have seen, are based on transcripts of Shakespeare's papers or of the prompt-book, and therefore a scribe might have modified the original markings. But, more than this, the printing-house changed such details. First, there may have been a 'house style', a general tendency in the printing-shop to punctuate (and spell) in certain ways regardless of the author's preferences. Then each compositor had favourite mannerisms: these can be traced by work on second editions where the copy from which the new text was set is available for comparison. Some compositors neglected commas; some frequently changed full-stops to colons or semi-colons; some added punctuation almost at random. These matters depended on personal taste, but also on the availability of type. Sometimes it is possible to calculate how many colons or commas were available to a compositor amongst his type and to observe where he ran short of one or the other and had to make substitutions. In the small printing-houses of Elizabethan London this often happened. The wonder is that the punctuation of their editions is as sensitive as it sometimes seems.

Three further factors modified the printed text. First, two compositors, with different habits and degrees of skill, sometimes worked on a single text. Secondly, the manuscript copy was sometimes marked (or 'cast-off' as it was called) so that the book could be set out of consecutive order: this could allow two compositors to work simultaneously and, more importantly, allow less type to stand, set-up, waiting to be placed in the printing machine. When the copy was cast-off in this way, it was sometimes done inaccurately so that the compositor had to spin out, or compress, some verse-lines towards the end of a page in order not to leave a space or over-run: so the verse arrangement could be seriously, and in very confusing ways, disturbed. Compositors also moved or modified stage-directions, or even omitted speeches, to the same end. Thirdly, the correction of proof-pages, when there was time for this, often introduced fresh errors. It was not often that the corrector referred back to the manuscript copy, so that he corrected only obvious errors, and only by his own sense of what was right. In this way punctuation, unusual words – and Shakespeare often invented words as he wrote – stage-directions, surprising speeches, could all be smoothed out of existence.

Clearly we must be careful in choosing what we ascribe to Shakespeare. For the closest examination, we must find 'good' passages from 'good' texts. We must pay no attention to the punctuation of modern editions, and treat that of the original editions with extreme scepticism or, where practicable, bibliographical expertise. Irregular arrangements of verse are significant only where there was no occasion for adjusting the cast-off copy; generally it is safe to accept a 'broken line' only where the metre seems to require it and no space on the original printed page has been saved or gained. [1]

Stage-directions and implications of stage activity in the dialogue require careful consideration too. Various manuscript plays have survived from Shakespeare's day (though no more than a few hundred lines of an unperformed play in Shakespeare's handwriting – the collaborative *Sir Thomas More*) and, from these and from printed plays, we know this: few scenes would be marked with a description of the location of the action; act or scene divisions would not always be marked; essential entries and exits, or directions for stage business, stage properties or costume changes might also be missing, misplaced or inaccurate. Plays printed from prompt-books were more consistent in marking entries; those from authorial manuscripts more descriptive in stage-directions. To gain a fair knowledge of what Shakespeare wanted to happen on the stage requires minute consideration of printed directions and textual inferences, together with a general knowledge of the Elizabethan playhouses and methods of play production.

This last requirement, in turn, requires practice and imagination, for Shakespeare's theatre is lost, of course, and must be reconstructed in our minds with as much co-ordination as possible. In my view, and in my experience of staging the plays, the most important features of that theatre were these:

The companies were permanent, run by eight to a dozen actors. They performed many different plays in repertory, rather like a modern opera company. They usually staged the plays in 'real' or modern dress – just extra-fine or apt versions of ordinary clothes; 'Roman' plays were something of an exception here. Music and rudimentary sound effects – drums

[1] Scholarly editions of Shakespeare's plays, such as the Arden, Signet or New Penguin (or the more recent volumes of the New Cambridge Edition), give accounts of the authority of their texts. For a general view of the subject see W. W. Greg, *The Shakespeare First Folio* (Oxford University Press, 1955).

and thunder, shouts, funeral or wedding bells – were often used. The light was daylight, or candles and torches in the few enclosed theatres; towards the end of a play, as daylight began to weaken in their usual winter afternoon performances, torch-light became more effective for contrasts. Movable scenery was provided chiefly in the form of largish properties: tombs, thrones, arbours, trees, prisoner's bar. The action took place on a squarish platform, surrounded on three or four sides by the audience. In the large public theatres the fourth side had a permanent background with doors, windows, alcove or balconies, which could be used for entries and exits, and for other incidents of the play's action; but the basic location of the play was the cleared space, in size some forty foot by thirty foot. Here the grouping of actors, the isolation of one or two, the costumes they wore, the hand-properties they carried (plays often demand sword, torch, prayer-book, bed, crown and so forth) and the gestures they used (wringing of hands, kneeling, kissing, running, 'making a stand' are often called for) were the dominant features of changing visual effects, given a focus by the frame and background of the unchanging platform.

The actors were thus, in every way, the centre of the theatre. John Webster, Shakespeare's contemporary, saw the actor as the centre of a circle, the lines of focus from the audience being so many radiuses from circumference to centre.

This kind of theatre encourages histrionic, realistic, personal drama: the confrontation of mighty or subtle opposites, or the laying bare of the inmost part of man. It also serves procession, pageantry, dance and an impression of dangerous confusion, as the acting area is filled with many supernumeraries. Always the appearance of the actor, his performance, his relation to others (and to empty space, doors or meaningful properties), are of prime importance, unsubdued and unemphasized by the elabor-ate scenery and expressive lighting effects that we are used to in modern theatres. Because these were the only important elements, all the Elizabethan and Jacobean companies toured frequently, readily transporting their plays from public playhouses to private ones, and to Court. In summer, when the London theatres were closed for fear of the plague, they were forced to travel further, to inn yards and the halls of great houses in the country. Costumes, portable properties, some music and actors moving and speaking in space made up the performance, without much further aid.[1]

The audience of course was important. In the public theatres many stood to watch the play, and all were in the same light as the actors. To hold attention performances would have to be strong; pace, rhythm and metrical basis of speech would have to be firmly controlled: energy, flexibility, clarity and personalities open to their audience were required. The prologue to *Henry V* is fanciful, but it conjures up a picture of dynamic production:

> O for a muse of fire, that would ascend
> The brightest heaven of invention;
> A kingdom for a stage, princes to act,
> And monarchs to behold the swelling scene.

The word 'monarch' reminds us of another huge difficulty in considering Shakespeare's plays from any point of view: they were written in and for a society different from our own. The divine right of kings, the importance of a hereditary class-structure, a police-state with censorship, informers, and summary imprisonment, religious certitude in dogmatic and expedient variety, and money made of gold were all accepted features of English life. Europe was moving slowly from feudal to capitalist structure. Empirical science was in its infancy and the 'ancients' still authoritative for many thinkers.

We can never respond to the plays as did Shakespeare's audiences. The wonder is that we respond, in our own way, so

[1] An account of the theatre buildings in which Shakespeare's plays were first performed, that is both responsible and imaginative, is C. Walter Hodges, *The Globe Restored: A Study of the Elizabethan Theatre* (Oxford University Press, 1953). For theatre practice in his time the most enlightening book is Bernard Beckerman, *Shakespeare at the Globe: 1599–1609* (Collier Macmillan, 1962). On acting, see John Russell Brown, *Shakespeare's Plays in Performance* (Arnold, 1966).

readily. I see two reasons for this: one, Shakespeare was prophetic of the social and intellectual changes then only just beginning; and two, the focus of the theatre on the actor encouraged dramatists to concentrate attention on individual men as physical, mental and temperamental realities. The bare stage had a test-tube simplicity: it isolated man as a living substance and sentient being, so that his actions and reactions could be clearly viewed. Those parts of human reality which for Elizabethan actors and audience, and for ourselves, are the most unchanging in their nature and operation, were thrown into relief by this theatre-form and, with lively and brilliant delineation, Shakespeare brought them into dramatic conflict and, sometimes, dramatic resolution. In seeking to open our imaginations to Shakespeare's creative work, we do well to concentrate upon space, time, his actors and his characters, and ourselves as reflected in that man-centred theatre.

3 The Theatrical Life in Shakespeare's Words

WE CANNOT read Shakespeare better simply by following a set of rules: the process is no mere computer-exercise. It has two stages. The first is to consider ways, as many of them as possible, in which we can respond, and to practise each almost for its own sake. So our powers of perception will be developed and strengthened. But this is only like practising scales, or staking claims to new territory. The next stage is assimilation, or taking possession of the territory.

Usually the two stages in acquiring an individual reading-method should go on side by side. The whole process is something like learning a new language. Grammar and vocabulary must be understood and learnt, and are the same for all beginners; but speaking is a more personal matter that needs practice and familiarity. The time comes when the grammar has become an unconscious basis for speech and for thought itself. So with learning to read Shakespeare.

In this chapter I will set out the basic elements of response as far as I recognize them in my own practice. And in the rest of the book I will, as it were, talk, try to respond to various passages as well as I am able and only by the way draw precise attention to the means I am using. To continue the metaphor of speech: the aim of this book is to increase the range and sensitivity of the language of theatrical response. Or to take the metaphor a step further, the aim is to encourage individual dialogues with Shakespeare's works.

I. WORDS

A straightforward beginning is to take the individual words, one at a time. This is appropriate for a careful response to any piece of writing. Questions to ask are:

How many nouns? abstract or concrete? What kind of things, activities or concepts do they represent; what is the range of their immediate reference? (We may find for example that political, religious, social, domestic, emotional, intellectual, sensory, or physical references predominate.) Are the nouns Saxon or Romance words? from Old English, or from French, Italian and classical originals?

How many verbs? active or passive, personal or impersonal? What tenses are used? What kinds of activity are represented?

How many adjectives? How many adverbs? How many negatives, comparatives, superlatives? How many personal pronouns, possessive, demonstrative, relative? How many participles, prepositions, conjunctions? and what kinds?

Describing vocabulary without concern for the meaning of words as parts of a whole is a surprisingly useful first step: it reveals the field of thought and sensation, the weight and muscularity of verbal expression. If the passage being considered is divided between two or more speakers, or is clearly organized in more than one section, analytical comparisons between the parts will sharpen awareness. If the field of reference changes during the scene, this is an important indication of the development of the passage: or if the word used for any one person, object, place or activity changes. (Variations in the name by which one person is addressed is a common device for indicating changed relationships between characters.)

The next step will concern syntax and construction:

How long, simple or complicated, are the sentences?

Are there many repetitions of words, phrases, or sentence-structures?

Where are dependent clauses placed, and what kinds predominate?

What figures of speech are used?

At this stage, before even looking at the meaning of what is communicated, we should heed specifically theatrical qualities: the sound of the words when spoken. It helps, I think, to listen for this before considering the audible effects of an actor's interpretation of character and involvement, or the demands of the dramatic context in terms of action and over-all timing. The requirements of the words themselves, as sound, should remain a part of the total heard experience of the play in performance. Perhaps it is easiest to begin with texture. Listen to the words spoken without being conscious of meaning, as if hearing a foreign language:

Do front or back vowels predominate? in particular places, or throughout? Are any consonants, or groups of consonants, especially recurrent?

Timing is of prime importance, and for this we must look to syntax and not the punctuation of original or modern editions:

How does the syntax (and necessary punctuation) break the utterance into units? How long or short are they, and is there a recurrent pattern in their variations which establishes a basic rhythm? Do the time-units suggested by the syntax vary in a consistent way? What units stand out against a basic pattern or sequence?

Does the speech fall into paragraphs, or clear groups of sentences, that likewise establish an identifiable pattern in sound?

Sentence-structure is the controlling factor here, together with the placing of monosyllabic as against polysyllabic nouns and verbs, and of relative clauses or adverbial phrases.

The duration of each unit and the varying density and texture of sound often reveal clear rhythmic patterns or structures, but for much of Shakespeare's writing a metrical basis for speech gives a further control of phrasing, timing and rhythm, and of stress or point. There are very sophisticated ways of discussing verse and various rules for speaking it, but for Shakespeare it is helpful to start as an Elizabethan would do. For him the iambic pentameter was a clear, consistent basis for versification. Unskilful dramatists made it ring out regularly ('tee-tum, tee-tum, tee-tum, tee-tum, tee-tum'), so that Thomas Nashe called it the 'drumming decasyllabon'. Spoken continuously in regular fashion this 'blank' verse form is boring and petty; but when the words are arranged so that they subtly depart from and return to this pattern, the disturbance and reassertion of the basic rhythm introduces tension, expectation, withholding or onward pressure, syncopation, speed, lightness, firmness and countless other aural effects. Elizabethan dramatists accepted the iambic pentameter, almost like a beat in music.[1] Two accounts are well known. First, Joseph Hall's in his satires, *Virgidemiarum* (1598), one of which pictures some dramatists following a play-text as if it were a musical score:

> Meanwhile our poets in high parliament,
> Sit watching every word, and gesturement,
> Like curious censors of some doughty gear,
> Whispering their verdict in their fellow's ear.
> Woe to the word whose margent in their scroll
> Is noted with a black condemning coal.
> But if each period might the synod please –
> Ho! bring the ivy boughs, and bands of bays.

Later, in a prologue to his play *If It Be Not Good, The Devil Is In It* (1612), Thomas Dekker claimed that a good playwright could secure attention and admiration by the musical harmony of his writing, irrespective of what the audience understood of his meaning: he can

> . . . call the banish'd auditor home, and tie
> His ear, with golden chains, to his melody:
> Can draw with adamantine pen even creatures

[1] Dorothy L. Sipe has recently proved Shakespeare's reliance on the simple iambic norm by a scientific investigation of word variants in the plays; see her *Shakespeare's Metrics* (1968).

Forg'd out of the hammer, on tiptoe to reach up
And, from rare silence, clap their brawny hands,
To applaud what their charm'd soul scarce understands.

Verse, for Elizabethans, was a 'certain' or fixed structure.
Samuel Daniel, poet and dramatist, wrote that 'all verse is but a
frame of words confined within certain measure, differing from
ordinary speech, and introduced the better to express men's
concepts both for delight and memory'. For an appreciation of
the effects of verse, each syllable should be related to the iambic
scheme. As Sir Philip Sidney put it:

> The senate of poets hath chosen verse as their fittest raiment...
> not speaking (table-talk fashion or like men in a dream) words as
> they chanceably fall from the mouth, but peysing [or weighing]
> each syllable of each word by just proportion according to the
> dignity of the subject.

Besides such control of weight or stress, verse also created that
music or harmony which Dekker believed could control an
unruly audience by its own attraction. Sidney agreed: 'the ex-
quisite observing of number and measure in words . . . did seem
to have some divine force in it'. Daniel called it: 'so natural a
melody . . ., and so universal, as it seems to be generally born with
all the nations of the world, as an hereditary eloquence proper to
all mankind'. Such claims for verse remind us of Shakespeare's
account of music in *The Merchant of Venice*:

> Therefore the poet
> Did feign that Orpheus drew trees, stones, and floods;
> Since nought so stockish, hard, and full of rage,
> But music for the time doth change his nature.
> The man that hath no music in himself,
> Nor is not moved with concord of sweet sounds,
> Is fit for treasons, stratagems, and spoils;
> The motions of his spirit are dull as night,
> And his affections dark as Erebus:
> Let no such man be trusted.   (V. i. 79–88)

Although we must consider the individual and momentary
effects of the sound of words over against the metrical basis, a

wide view should be sustained as well. A constant interplay has been created between the rhythmic organization of syntax and word-positioning and that of the metre, so that effects are developed over whole paragraphs. There may be a sequence in which syntax fits neatly with verse-lines, each iambic pentameter concluding with a full-stop or colon; then a line may follow in which the syntax clearly suggests three breaks in utterance within the single pentameter. Or a mid-line break, or caesura, may be present in each line, varying its position until, perhaps, a line comes with no break at all. By such means, firm continuity, or hesitation, or gathering energy, for example, can be conveyed by sound. When Shakespeare required more thorough changes in sound patterns, he varied the basic blank verse with various kinds of rhymed verse, especially couplets, or with octosyllabics, alexandrines, short prose passages and so forth. All these changes must be noted with regard to their sequence, for with consideration of sound we are already involved with drama as a continuous experience in time.

At this point, too, we must begin to consider meaning, for as the verse-form interacts with syntax and word-positioning to create an effective 'musical' sound, so that music interacts with the meaning of the words. This point can scarcely be made without examining a short passage as example. Consider Viola's soliloquy towards the end of *Twelfth Night*, in which meaning is clearly expressed:

> He named Sebastian. I my brother know
> Yet living in my glass; even such and so
> In favour was my brother, and he went
> Still in this fashion, colour, ornament,
> For him I imitate. O, if it prove,
> Tempests are kind and salt waves fresh in love.
>
> (III. iv. 3 54 ff.)

Each of the first three lines has an unmistakable break, moving progressively nearer the line-ending. Line 4 has two slighter breaks towards the end. Line 5 has its major break, with a firm ending to a sentence, aft er the sixth syllable, and then a change of

address, with perhaps a further slight pause after the first inarticulate syllable. Then the last line has no necessary break, although the
Folio text does mark a comma after *kind*; some slight change of
pitch or emphasis is required here, if not a pause. The vocabulary
is unremarkable except in the last line; and here the uniquely
sustained sound, the almost regular beat on each of the five
syllables stressed by the metre – *Temp-*, *kind*, *salt*, *fresh*, and
love – together with the manner in which *waves* attracts emphasis
in spite of the fully provided metre, gives to this line assured and
abundant energy. The effect clearly depends on the relation of
this line to all the others in the soliloquy. Compare the other
nouns, verbs and personal pronouns with something of the same
unequivocal metrical stress: *He* or *named*, *I*, *broth-*, *know*, *liv-*, *glass*,
such, *so*, *fav-*, *was*, *bro-*, *Still*, *fash-*, *col-*, *orn-*, *him*, *if*, *prove*;
Sebastian, *ornament* and *imitate* are polysyllables that can carry only
one major stress and yet occupy more than one iambic foot, so
that there is some doubt how, exactly, they should be stressed. At
the most, there are four clear monosyllabic stresses to the lines,
until the full-fraught, resonant and resolving last line, which
brims over and yet still manages, by means of rhyme and a slight
mid-line pause, to give special emphasis to *kind* and *love*. *Prove*,
too, of the preceding line, is given an unforced significance by
returning to a regular stress after the reversed foot (tum-tee, tee-
tum) and as the hinge point in the rhythmic design. Mark on the
page the clear stresses of this speech, compare them with an
absolutely regular iambic metre, modify the stress to be used so
that the natural pronunciation is as close to the iambic pentameter
as possible, and then speak it aloud. You will find that both
meaning and sound have become clearer, working together: in
effect, the speech is both a 'concord of sweet sounds' and a
meaningful account of Viola's thoughts; it 'peyses' the weight of
each syllable, 'according to the dignity of the subject'.

   Texture, too, has a part in the interplay of sound and sense. For
instance, there are few back vowels in this passage and they,
mostly *o*'s and *u*'s, are grouped towards the ends of lines. The
penultimate line marks this most clearly with the stressed *O* and

prove, which are not echoed until the whole resolves and con-cludes with the rhyme on *love*. The *T* of *Tempests* in the last line, together with the reversal of its iambic foot, helps to give an impression of urgent feeling breaking through, for no other word in the passage starts with this letter: the effect is reinforced by the similarity of the two vowels in this word, its further *t* and two *s*'s. The sound of this word disturbs the expectations that the earlier sounds have aroused. Its vowel is echoed in the second part of the line with *fresh*; yet, because of the slight metrical irregu-larity and the absence of a verb, this syllable has its own energy and responds only slightly to the connection backwards. The unusual (in this passage) vowel of *salt* helps the resolving rhythm and prevents the parallel structure of the last line from sounding too pat. The conclusion of the soliloquy seems alight with energy, dancingly afloat, as well as being a firm conclusion in metre and meaning.

The example I have chosen hardly begins to reveal the problems of meaning or communication that Shakespeare's mature writing often poses, and to which a theatrical reading of the text must now proceed to give attention. On the literary level, these have often been studied, so that it is common knowledge that, by the use of similes, metaphors, personifications and other forms of imagery, Shakespeare created a complex expression of thought and feeling. When a character talks about politics, he may use a train of imagery suggesting bestial activity and revulsion; talking of the activity of another person, his words may suggest his own physical tension, or sensitivity, or intellectualization. Speech in Shakespeare carries trains of allusive feeling or thought along with its ostensible denotive meaning; it is like a ship that raises a wake, beside and behind it, which animates thoughts and sensations often far removed from its direct course.

The last line of the passage just discussed brings with it allusions to vastness, power, death and sorrow; it calls on sensa-tions of vision, taste, touch and sound that depend on experience outside that which is directly represented on the stage. The inter-play is subtle, for with *Tempest*, *salt*, *waves* and *fresh* come the contrastingly effective words that relate personally to Viola: 'kind' and 'love'. Earlier only *glass* had anything like a comparable allusiveness; but this may be important in suggesting brittleness and the mere reflection of an impression.

The word 'kind', in this context we have examined, can have two meanings: 'gentle' and 'natural'. Often in Shakespeare such varying meanings are equally relevant, playing against each other; first one is dominant and then, as the sentence or speech develops, the other becomes more apposite. These puns allow a speaker to mean one thing and betray another; or to pretend one thing, and think or feel another. Not every pun is important, but when it is crucially placed, or is in a sequence of similar puns, or when it suits with the allusions of the imagery, then its validity is ensured.

In both punning and allusiveness each word must be evaluated in its context, and it is here that theatrical considerations come quickly into play:

Is the double meaning or allusion conscious or unconscious for the speaker? Does it augment or counterstate the prevalent line of expression? Does emotional meaning offset the intellectual, the individual offset the social or general?

These questions involve a consideration of speech as an expression of a person's involvement in a situation at a particular moment in time; or rather a partial expression, for physical appearance and being are also expressive, in the theatre as in life. We must ask not merely what the words say, directly and indirectly, but also:

What 'speaks' besides the words?

This involves action and performance.

But before considering this complication, the marshalling of speech between a number of persons must be analysed. In real life we know that the person who speaks most is not necessarily the dominant feature of a group: one participant may keep others in control by changing the topic of conversation; another by saying little, forcefully, or surprisingly, or by appealing to common interests rather than individual concerns; another may impress by a parade of detailed knowledge or the revelation of secret facts, or by keeping everyone else, in turn, pleased or curious. Strategic questions like these should be asked about Shakespeare's dialogue:

Is communication cumulative, or climactic, or digressive? Is it contained by antithesis or narrative?

Is surprise or expectation introduced? Is delay of satisfaction noticeable?

Are questions important, or exclamations?

Does the person (or persons) addressed change in the course of a single speech? Is there any soliloquy within dialogue? Is a soliloquy addressed to the audience, or no one, or an absent person?

Does one character dominate the dialogue, or is the 'lead' shared between several? Is the lead in conversation surprisingly or regularly passed from one to another?

The eyes of spectators in a theatre tend to be drawn to the dominant speaker, so exchange of lead is an effective means of concentrating attention, especially if one character consistently or surprisingly takes it from the others. To appreciate this factor differing degrees of knowledge or feeling must be analysed:

Does any speaker know more, or feel more, about the situation than the others? Is this expressed, directly or allusively, or punningly? Or is there no apparent expression?

Does the audience know more than all, or some, of the characters? Do the words sometimes allude to this knowledge without the speaker being aware of it?

Is any speaker noticeably silent, refusing to answer direct questions, or delaying an expected intervention?

Does anyone speak unnecessarily, without obvious motivation?

The basic concern is how the understanding of the audience and the focus of its attention are affected by the words as they are spoken in a group on stage. The analysis of dramatic style needs to account for structure, contrast, tension, climax, confusion, expectation, delay, satisfaction, inevitability, relaxation, and the concentration or dispersal of attention. Moreover drama communicates variously in time: it is dynamic, and continuously changing in its manner of drawing attention, and in its impression of total or partial statement. The analysis of theatre speech must account for all these qualities.

II. ACTION

The first step towards analysing what the sight of a play in performance communicates to an audience is to define what visual accompaniments to speech the text necessarily involves:

> What do the authoritative stage-directions say? Which characters are on stage? What movements, entries and exits are required? Are any gestures, costumes or properties specified? What kinds of movements and objects are there: domestic, formal, intimate, sensual?

For a Shakespeare play this enquiry will give only the barest facts. But if any author believed a visual device important there is a strong possibility that the words by which he communicated his notion of the play would hint at this, directly or indirectly. So we should ask:

> What actions, costumes or properties are implied by the dialogue? What kinds are there? Is any facial expression specified, or physical bearing?

Visual effects which are reinforced by spoken description or comment may well have added effectiveness in performance.

These questions will provide the basic details, but more may be deduced. It is important, considering the intense focus upon the actor provided by Elizabethan conditions of performance, to examine the text as a whole most carefully for inferences about

costume and behaviour. For analysing any one passage, simple
questions such as these are useful:

How old are the characters? How many of each sex? Who are
blood relatives?

What clothes are being worn, what properties carried?

How would the time of day or year, or the place where the
action takes place, alter bearing, behaviour or movement?

What changes in physical bearing, behaviour and tempo occur
during the scene? Or are there changes compared with each
character's previous entries on to the stage?

As we may consider speech as music, so action and visual effect
can usefully be described in dance-like terms. We must ask about
grouping:

Which characters would stand, or sit, close to each other? Is
there one group of figures, or more?

Does the grouping of figures remain essentially unchanged
throughout the scene?

A single excited character among others who are concerned with
routine matters will be an obvious focus of attention, and probably a disturbing one. Or only one character may be still in a
crowded scene; or two characters may draw together as others
disperse over the stage. We should ask:

Are there any contrasts in tempo, rhythm, movement, bearing
between individual figures? or between an individual and a
group, or between two or more groups?

Do the figures on stage change from individually appropriate
actions to concerted ones, or the other way about?

Concerted or group activity in Shakespeare's plays comes
most obviously with certain ritual situations: marriage, betrothal,
coronation, enthronement, prayer, celebratory dance, procession.
But entries and exits often provide similar opportunities, and also
scenes of consultation or debate.

As visual contrasts are important, so are repetitions. The eye takes in the stage at a glance so that a repetition of one grouping at various times in a play is a quick means of exposition; it is also capable of drawing attention to slight rearrangements indicative of changing involvements among the characters. We should ask:

Is the basic grouping (and activity) of the figures on stage repeated at any other time in the play and, if so, does this presentation differ from the others?

Interactions between speech and movement alter the effectiveness of both:

Does the physical performance and visual effect support the effect of words, or counterstate it? Does one particular character use action more than speech, or the other way about?

Are there moments when the spoken drama waits upon the physical and visual, or when the tempo of one, or its explicitness, exceeds that of the other? (An excited entry to a scene of deliberate debate is, for example, immediately effective.)

Are there moments of movement and no speech, or vice versa?

This last question is particularly important with a crowded stage, when even a short moment of silence or absolute stillness can create a great effect; the figure who causes the change or breaks through the silence gains immediate attention. A halt in exciting narrative or activity is likewise impressive, by contrasts of vision and sound.

Often a physical activity brings with it an aural accompaniment: the sound of footsteps, panting or deep breathing, sobs. These must be considered as they support or contrast the sound of speech, in volume, tempo, rhythm, pitch, texture, and so forth. At this stage, too, we should be careful to list all sound and light effects, and consider how they affect both the aural and visual impressions of the play in performance. For example a bright torch held close to someone's unmoving face could direct the audience's attention away from the speaker to the silent face; the flicker of the torch could subtly quicken the tempo. A general darkening of the stage could make the audience uncertain where to look, and this slight strain would tend to take attention away from the words. The sound of trumpets calling to battle off stage would either obliterate deliberate speech or else, with the actors speaking more loudly, make it sound still more controlled by contrast. Music played on or off stage obviously makes the greatest effect of this kind, but the sounds of rustling clothes or of swords in scabbards may be highly significant in certain specially prepared contexts.

III. PERFORMANCE

So far we have artificially separated words from action in order to clarify our view of the play in performance, but both of course are co-existent, springing from the single palpable reality of actors on a stage in consecutive events. The third series of questions joins speech to action in enquiring about the actor's task in staging the play. Of course each actor will respond in an individual way, according to his personal talents, his training and the company of which he is a member. But the demands upon actors and the decisions they have to face remain the same.

Besides asking what the words effect by themselves, the actor has to ask how they involve the character he represents:

Does the speaker say precisely what he means, or what he thinks he means? Are words his only reaction at this point? Does his choice of words, images, puns suggest a second reaction, or still more complicated reactions, alongside, or underneath, his obvious meaning? Is he conscious or unconscious of any or all of these various disparate reactions?

Why does he speak? Why now? Why in this way? Why to this person? Why is he silent? Why does he stop speaking, or change the subject or the person addressed?

The basic questions about his words any actor must ask are: why and how? or to what end, and how can I make it work?

An actor's ability to suggest that his character's involvement is at several levels of consciousness has been most clearly described in Stanislavski's account of 'subtext'. His books, translated as *An Actor Prepares*, *Building a Character* and *Creating a Role*, relate immediately to his work as an actor, director and teacher at the Moscow Art Theatre, but they have been recognized as the most comprehensive account available of the art of acting. This master has stated clearly that 'the text of a play is not valuable in and of itself, but is made so by the inner content of the subtext and what is contained in it'. Subtext he defines as

> the manifest, the inwardly felt expression of a human being in a part, which flows uninterruptedly beneath the words of the text, giving them life and a basis for existing. The subtext is a web of innumerable, varied inner patterns inside a play and a part, woven from 'magic ifs', given circumstances, all sorts of figments of the imagination, inner movements, objects of attention, smaller and greater truths and a belief in them, adaptations, adjustments and other similar elements. *It is the subtext that makes us say the words we do in a play.*[1]

By considering emotional, intellectual and physical performance as a support for the words, as *a way of making them necessary* in all their particularities, we can locate those moments when the text requires most subtextual support. It is here that Shakespeare has chosen to rely on subtext, to make it unmistakably effective. There are moments, and sometimes whole characters, where subtext is not significantly different from the text, where the actor's task is to support the exact words with as strong and complete a physical performance as possible: roles like 'Mercy' or 'Fury' in a medieval morality play, whose characteristics, unlike those of human beings, must be consistently in a single vein, are obvious examples.

When Shakespeare makes a character put on a disguise so that he pretends to be a different person, or to have purposes different from his true intentions, or to act in a play, there are obvious

[1] *Building a Character*, tr. Elizabeth R. Hapgood (1949 ed., Reinhart, 1950), pp. 114 and 113; italics mine.

moments when an inner, subtextual 'truth' breaks through the 'appearance': Rosalind pretending to be the voluble and unresponsive Ganymede faints as she sees Orlando's bloody handkerchief (*As You Like It*, IV. iii. 155); Macbeth speaking to Banquo about the witches' promise that he should be Thane of Cawdor, when his thoughts are clearly concerned with kingship and, probably, with murder (*Macbeth*, I. iii. 87). In the first of these examples the 'truth' is expressed through silence and physical performance; in the second, it is suggested or hinted at by the apparent inadequacy of the words. Such are some of the signs of subtextual pressures in roles which do not clearly involve disguise; and similar devices reveal the unconscious pressures within more obviously two-faced roles.

An actor can invent a subtext from his own repertoire of previous roles and foist it onto a text, bending the words to serve his own purposes. But a good text implies its own, proper subtext, the one which truly supports the words and is supported by them. Careful examination can show where subtext should become unambiguously manifest, or where the very consistency of a performance depends upon particular subtextual bridges or pressures. The clearest signs of subtextual manifestations are these:

A sudden, immediately inexplicable, change of subject, or of person addressed, or a refusal to change the subject of talk when this is expected.

A stylistic break-through, of vocabulary or rhythm or syntax, especially if the change is subsequently sustained, perhaps through a series of brief interruptions of the staple style.

A sequence of puns or images that suggest a preoccupation other than the ostensible ones of the speech, especially when this sequence grows in strength. (For Shakespeare this is the most common and noticeable manifestation of subtextual concerns, often revealing basic responses far from the conscious involvement of a character.)

A refusal to speak, especially when required by others or by circumstances to do so; or an avoidance of the clear naming of a matter of crucial importance; or the using of too many words for the subject in hand, the giving of too great attention to an apparently minor matter. (Sometimes extreme simplicity of verbal communication, a kind of verbal emptiness, indicates most strongly the need for the actor to impress the full force of feeling under the words, subtextually, by physical or nervous exhibition.)

A movement or gesture in the place of words, especially when it denies the tenor of words spoken just before or after. (Sometimes a physical or facial reaction, out of keeping with the impression of the words spoken, may be described subsequently by another character.)

An eccentric, unusual or apparently too powerful word, especially when its echo is picked up later by some other sign of subtextual activity.

Asides, or soliloquies, that reveal thoughts not overtly expressed in the preceding dialogue. Or flat contradictions in dialogue, of which the speaker does not seem to be aware.

As we identify the moments where the actor has to make an impression not immediately explicit in the words he speaks, we define the nature of the subtextual support that is called for by the text.

I think that two comments should be made here. First, that even when subtext makes a statement contrary to the simple meaning of the words, it does not work against the words. The actor's opportunity is suggested by the words, and the subtextual element of his performance achieves effectiveness in large part by the context provided by the verbal drama; so to become aware of subtext is to increase one's awareness of the dramatic life implicit in the printed words. Text and subtext are two expressive manifestations of a single dramatic consciousness which can never be fully explicit in a printed book.

The second comment is that, while an actor is skilled at discovering how to fill out his performance 'under the words', a reader of the text is not wholly at a disadvantage in comparison with him. The actor will always think in terms of what he himself can do on the stage, with his particular physique and temperament; this will limit the freedom with which he studies the text for its own – and Shakespeare's – sake. If a reader learns to project himself into the dialogue, so that in his imagination he sees and feels himself trying to make the words necessary in all their complexity and in their unalterable sequence, he may offset inexperience and absence from the stage with a fuller exploration and a more patient waiting for the words to reveal their own hidden potentiality.

Shakespeare has been famed for centuries as a creator of character and of a lively image of life. This achievement is in large part due to his ability to imagine total human reactions and write down words that give actors and readers the power to recreate from the words that full reality: verbal utterance in his plays is part of a complicated illusion of life. For these reasons any analysis of Shakespeare's dramatic style must pay strict – that is textually based – attention to subtext.

A further aspect of the actor's task, the shaping of a performance as a whole, is not so readily considered by a reader but is absolutely required for a proper performance and is therefore an element of dramatic style. The varied details of textual and subtextual interpretation have to be controlled so that nothing is given too great or too little importance. When a reader considers the complications of the text, this is easily forgotten.

Usually the shape or proportion of a performance is worked out partly by an actor's intuitive understanding and his sense of his own capabilities, and partly by experiment during extensive rehearsals. Stanislavski spoke of the over-all shaping of performances and productions in terms of 'through-line' and 'super-objective':

> In a play the whole stream of individual, minor objectives, all the imaginative thoughts, feelings and actions of an actor, should converge to carry out the *super-objective* of the plot. The common bond must be so strong that even the most insigni-

ficant detail, if it is not related to the *super objective*, will stand
out as superfluous or wrong.[1]

Stanislavski tried to control the shape of a performance and production by his view of the play's plot, of what happens in the
play. This is obviously a major concern, but in Shakespeare's
closely imagined texts there are other, more local signs, of what
should be *forte*, what *piano*, where the climaxes should be placed,
what the scale should be, how fully involved the actor should
become, and so forth. In considering the style of any passage from
this point of view the following questions are useful:

> How relevant is this to the principal action of the play? How
> often and where are its words or activities repeated elsewhere
> in the play? How strong or weak are its rhythms in comparison
> with other passages?
>
> Is the development simple or diverse? Is significant narrative
> information given here? Is any expectation satisfied or further
> delayed in the course of the scene?
>
> Does the speech of the passage become simpler or more com-
> plicated? How do its rhythms change? Do subtextual impres-
> sions become textual? Is the dominant effect aural or visual,
> group or individual?
>
> Is the passage essentially an encounter between two characters,
> and if so is there a change of power between them, and where
> and by what means is this effected?
>
> Does the passage include a climactic revelation of a character's
> involvement in the action, and if so, by what means is this
> effected?

Of these questions I believe the last to be especially important for
Shakespeare's dramatic writing, for the impress of living people is
a primary fact of the plays in performance, and his basic strategy
is to reveal progressively the grounds of character. For a small
character, like William in *As You Like It*, we can see this working
in a single scene; for the larger ones, earlier scenes complicate and

[1] *An Actor Prepares*, tr. Elizabeth R. Hapgood (1937, ed. 1959), p. 271.

confuse the audience's perception, and later ones establish the dominant features, some of which were almost hidden at first. Once a play is known in general outline, a good way to study an individual role is to trace it backwards from the fifth Act to the first.

None of these questions will give a simple definition of a character's 'through-line', or of a play's 'super-objective', of the sort that Stanislavski encouraged his actors to seek. (And it is questionable whether any single formulation is appropriate for Shakespeare's plays.) But such questions do indicate what are the main forces of dramatic interest in any one passage of a play, where the effective and developing energy can be located.

How an actor creates his role in detail will vary from man to man, and each will highlight certain moments. With Shakespeare's plays the salient fact here is the way in which they seem to accommodate so many and so various talents. In reading a text this can hardly be grasped, but some notion is better than none and some experiment is advisable. Take a short speech (or if possible share a duologue with someone else), learn it by heart, and then try various quite arbitrary changes in delivery: loud then soft; slow then quick; arranged in long phrases and then short; high and then low in pitch; rough and then smooth in texture. If a duologue is being spoken, change between each speech; if a soliloquy, change with each sentence or clause, or start quickly and finish slowly, and then the other way round. Activity can be introduced, such as moving during speech, sitting instead of standing, and so on. These are exploratory exercises: some will sound nonsensical and absurd, but some few may reveal new and unexpected ways of making the speech sound both effective and true. Introduce an audience – one is enough – and ask for his response to each manner of performance, immediately after each is completed; or tape-record a selection of different renderings and hear and judge them for yourself a week or so later. This exercise can become less arbitrary, so that three or four contrary and plausible interpretations are developed. Then, by trying to decide which fits most satisfactorily with the dramatic style of the passage, something of the actor's opportunity and freedom of choice may be understood. There is an openness, an invitation for individual, personal enactment, in Shakespeare's dramatic writing that can be appreciated only by some such active experiment.

But one further effect of performance which is reflected in the style of each passage cannot be grasped by a reader without long experience. Needless to say, it is the element that is the hardest of all to grasp even in practical theatre work: the corporate dramatic energy. We can trace individual roles so much easier than the ensemble effects that depend on the contributions of many individuals, each modified by those of their fellows. Some questions may be useful:

Do all the characters think or feel alike at any one moment? Do they almost do so, and what are the exceptions?

Are there moments when interest, verbal or visual, is clearly focused on one particular word or on one point of the stage? Are there moments when interest seems particularly unfocused, so that any word or point may take attention for a brief moment and immediately lose it? Does attention ever seem held by the general picture rather than by any individual or group of figures? Does the focus suddenly change from a wide view to a narrow, or the other way around?

How much could an audience laugh? Why would they laugh?

How much could an audience cry, or feel close to tears? Why would they so sympathize?

When, and by what means, might the play make the audience remember, precisely and consciously, their own individual lives during the performance? Are they made to think, with some particularity and for some length of time, about the consequences of the actions represented on the stage in other situations, or for other persons, and if so, by what means?

Are any abstract, or generally valid, ideas presented so that the audience might consider them outside their immediate dramatic context, and if so, by what means?

At this point it is well for Hamlet's words to end the list of questions, for they certainly are comprehensive:

> How does the play serve 'the purpose of playing, whose end, both at the first and now, was and is to hold, as 'twere, the mirror up to nature; to show virtue her own feature, scorn her own image, and the very age and body of the time his form and pressure'?

IV. IMAGE OF LIFE

From the most detailed and technical analysis that we can manage, we must return at the end of our reading of a play to the widest of questions:

> What do we see of ourselves in this play?
>
> Do we find ourselves transformed in its image, or are we made conscious of ourselves as contrasted with the image of human life on the stage?
>
> How deeply have we observed the hidden motivations of persons and the hidden forces in the sequence of events portrayed on the stage?
>
> What fantasy, simplification, exaggeration, precise reality have we shared or observed?
>
> What satisfactions, doubts, questions, excitements and frustrations have we experienced?
>
> What 'truth', what 'beauty', have we recognized?
>
> How is our appreciation of life enhanced, or experience and understanding of it increased?

These are the perennial questions of criticism. The purpose of the smaller, more manageable questions that are considered in this book is to help in posing these large questions, to help us know what we are talking about when we consider the theatrical life of Shakespeare's plays.

PART TWO

1 Romeo and Juliet

WRITTEN about 1595, some five years after Shakespeare had become established as a playwright in London, *Romeo and Juliet* is a controlled and elaborate work that has been successful in the theatre from its earliest days until the present. Its hero and heroine are now famous throughout the world, and many playwrights, composers and choreographers have been inspired to create on the same theme and often within the same narrative structure.

A consideration of Shakespeare's dramatic style may profitably begin here. Many of the play's most effective scenes are focused on one or two characters, so that the situations are often visually simple, and comparatively simple psychologically. The language, however, is complicated by numerous images, comparisons and other figures of speech, is clearly related to the iambic pentameter and often uses rhyme. With this obviously artificial medium, Shakespeare has created characters with lively and deep involvement in their story so that an audience responds readily to them, as if they were living beings. The contrived – the poetic – nature of Shakespeare's drama is evident.

Passages have been chosen for analysis that take advantage of this dramatic simplicity. So there is nothing from the Nurse or Mercutio, characters who look forward to later subtleties in speech and psychological verisimilitude. Only the lines quoted from the very end of the play call for an appreciation of a group or large ensemble effect.

The predominant concern in this chapter will be with words, but words as spoken and heard, and as part of an individual performance. Later chapters will widen the perspective. In all the following chapters, the commentary is designed to be read with continuous reference to the passages quoted.

PROLOGUE

CHORUS: Two households both alike in dignity,
 In fair Verona where we lay our scene,
From ancient grudge break to new mutiny,
 Where civil blood makes civil hands unclean.
From forth the fatal loins of these two foes   5
 A pair of star-crossed lovers take their life;
Whose misadventured piteous overthrows
 Doth with their death bury their parents' strife.
The fearful passage of their death-marked love,
 And the continuance of their parents' rage,   10
Which, but their children's end, nought could remove,
 Is now the two hours' traffic of our stage;
The which if you with patient ears attend,
What here shall miss, our toil shall strive to mend.

                Exit

The tragedy of *Romeo and Juliet* starts with this Prologue. Visual drama and acting opportunities are limited here, so that enquiry must centre attention on words and metre. Yet other elements must not be forgotten: as the single figure enters to speak on behalf of the actors' company, he has to take command of the stage; and when he has gained the attention of his audience, he speaks of 'dignity'. So, with his 'stage-presence' as well as his words, he creates a living image of authority and decorum. He establishes a sample, or starter, for the main dramatic reality to follow; it is centred on individual performance, the mystery and challenge of one figure that commands silence.

The first line runs firmly within the frame of an iambic pentameter, and the following one, with a reference to fellow players, has absolute regularity. In these two lines, only 'dignity', having little stress on its final two syllables, gives a slight variation from the iambic norm; but this is soon balanced by the regular second line. The fourteen lines of the Prologue are so rhymed that they form a sonnet, with three quatrains and a concluding couplet, so that this nearly regular start is part of an impression of over-all control.

Perhaps the last syllables of 'dignity' were pronounced more fully in Shakespeare's time, for such words were sometimes rhymed with 'eye' or 'I'; but the lightness of its first two vowels is undoubted and, in contrast with the preceding vowels, they make this word a little less secure than its neighbours. The slight suggestion of imbalance is followed by a decisive disturbance of the iambic form in 'break' of line 3, which is placed where there should normally be an unstressed syllable. In the same line, 'grudge', a personal, almost individual reaction, is teamed with 'mutiny', held up by the rhyme and introducing a reference to large issues of warfare and insurrection. In the fourth line, 'civil' is used twice, punningly, so that a similar, but reversed, opposition is effected with a single word: first it refers to civil war, and then to civil manners; conflict and then the actual, individual, fair-seeming 'hands' of those responsible for the bloodshed. The metre is still remarkably regular, although 'makes' probably attracts some stress, as well as the five regularly stressed syllables, by reason of its likeness to 'break' of the preceding line, in sound, grammatical strength and metrical position. By these metrical and verbal niceties, Shakespeare ensured that, if the first quatrain is spoken with regard for its metrical form, it will have a contained power, an impression of disruptive energy consciously restrained within set form – 'dignity' and its antithesis 'mutiny'. But all this is effected with sufficient ease for containing the gentle, euphonious regularity of the second line.

The second quatrain (lines 5–8) introduces new themes: fate and sexuality, sustained by alliteration on 'f' and 'l', the 'f' also connecting 'fatal' with 'foe' and the now continuous theme of warfare. (This military reference is pointed by rhymes on 'over-throws' and 'strife'.) At first there is a renewed metrical regularity, but the sense begins to move in larger units than the ten-syllabled lines, line 5 being the first without punctuation at the end: ideas thus seem to outgrow their earlier bounds. Epithets, too, have new strength of sound and sense. The now famous 'star-crossed' and 'misadventure' may well have been coined by Shakespeare for this passage, since the *New English Dictionary* records both here for the first time and follows this quotation with imitative passages from later dramas. The fully-laden line 7 contains only one unit of thought, where all the previous lines have two; but the slight pause required in mid-line, to prevent the two epithets colliding, gives it a more impulsive rhythm. Again there is a run-over of sense to line 8, which starts with the verb of the sentence, a stronger link than that between lines 5 and 6. The first foot of line 8 is reversed, so that it is 'death' on the fourth syllable that secures both metre and sense. Yet, as soon as this is effected, immediately there is a misplaced stress on 'bury' which is like that on 'break' in line 3, only more strongly placed because of the initial irregularity and the fact that this line must conclude a quatrain. Now, in this section of the Prologue, speech has stronger currents and more urgent energy. Perhaps all its meanings or suggestions are not fully resolved: the physicality of 'loins', underlying its heraldic usage, remains unechoed, unless in 'bury'; and, if 'take' echoes the earlier 'break' and 'makes' strongly enough, there could be an element of subtextual ambiguity, for the usual, active connotations of this verb (which these other verbs provoke) can make the phrase mean 'take their death', rather than their 'birth'.

The third quatrain brings a third compound epithet, 'death-marked', again without earlier citation in the *New English Dictionary*. And, as at the opening of the second quatrain, a new theme or reaction is introduced with 'fearful', an elaboration perhaps of the previous 'fatal' which is more clearly developed in 'death-marked' with its ominous allusion to the more usual 'birth-marked'. The words 'passage' and 'continuance' stand out from the others in being partly abstract in reference; and the contrast between them – the temporary and the permanent – has an effect like the contrasts between earlier pairs of words, only now the influence extends over two lines. Then rhythm is sharpened, in line 11, by syntax and word-order which demand two pauses if the sense is to be made clear. As this line steadies itself on the concluding rhyme, there comes the first negative of the whole speech: 'which, but their children's end, nought could remove'.

After strongly stating themes, situation and narrative, the speaker now awakens fear, anticipation, expectation, unsatisfied curiosity; he becomes at once more lively and more withholding or mysterious. Then, for the first time since line 2, he reminds the audience of the actors and their stage. Possibly the word 'traffic' (or business) is self-deprecatory; certainly it develops references implicit in 'passage' and 'continuance'. The speaker of the prologue, who had seemed to know all and had controlled his announcement with antitheses, metre and rhyme, now suggests that the play's action is ordinary, limited in scope, general in energy. Again he awakens curiosity, by a dramatic withholding of the fiery speech towards which his earlier words had seemed to be progressively leading.

The last couplet picks up interest quickly and lightly with the comprehensive 'The which', and the first (and last) reference to the audience. Although 'you' is firmly placed at the fourth syllable, it is preceded by an 'if' and waits for its verb until the end of the line. The relationship between the speaker and his audience changes for these last two lines; but there is no relaxation, or quickening, of pace; no sharing of a point of view or of reaction. He is both more aware of them and more distant from them. He is closer to the actual beginning of the play, for instead of 'our scene' or 'our stage', he speaks now of 'here'; the tense has moved from present to future; and 'miss' could easily refer to the actors' expertise, their efficiency in the 'traffic' of the stage. Yet an ambiguity comes from a possible echo of '*mis*adventure' and the openness of 'What': 'what here shall miss' could refer not to the performance, but to the author's imagination, the events shown, or the audience's reaction. The word 'strive' looks back to 'strife' in the rhyme of line 8; and 'mend' to 'break' (3) and to that chain of words which relates to destruction and disorder. Possibly 'miss', 'toil' and 'mend' also reflect 'nought could remove'.

The sonnet form, the generally regular metre and the comparative brevity and packed exposition of the prologue, alike encourage a slow, deliberate delivery in which such reflections between words might have opportunity to work in the speaker's delivery and the audience's awareness. The sonnet form recommended itself to Elizabethan poets for just such complex completeness, for its ability to express, at one and the same time, self-awareness, self-criticism, and self-concealment. The play has seemed to grow in the speaker's mind until he has to hold back from telling what he knows; and, then, in the last metrically fluent couplet, the success of the whole venture of performance and acceptance becomes an open question:

> The which if you with patient ears attend,
> What here shall miss, our toil shall strive to mend.

The drama which follows is to be powerful and fateful, and yet, like an open question, it awaits a willing attention and responsible judgement.

When his speech is finished, the Prologue must walk off stage, and the audience is left to 'attend' to the play. At once there is a contrast, a boisterous entrance of two serving-men, speaking prose with no 'dignity' at all and refusing 'toil': 'Gregory, on my word we'll not carry coals.' Mutiny presses forward as the controlled, single voice finishes. The sonnet has its own mysterious energy and, seemingly from deep within the speaker's controlling mind, the play and its dominant themes seem to spring to life and await response.

Act II, Scene ii

ROMEO: He jests at scars that never felt a wound.

Enter JULIET *above*

> But soft, what light through yonder window breaks?
> It is the east, and Juliet is the sun.
> Arise fair sun and kill the envious moon,
> Who is already sick and pale with grief   5
> That thou her maid art far more fair than she.
> Be not her maid since she is envious.
> Her vestal livery is but sick and green,
> And none but fools do wear it; cast it off.

It is my lady, O it is my love.   10
O that she knew she were.
She speaks, yet she says nothing. What of that?
Her eye discourses, I will answer it.
I am too bold, 'tis not to me she speaks.
Two of the fairest stars in all the heaven,   15
Having some business, do entreat her eyes
To twinkle in their spheres till they return.
What if her eyes were there, they in her head?
The brightness of her cheek would shame those stars,
As daylight doth a lamp; her eyes in heaven   20
Would through the airy region stream so bright
That birds would sing, and think it were not night.
See how she leans her cheek upon her hand.
O that I were a glove upon that hand,
That I might touch that cheek.
JULIET: Ay me!
ROMEO: She speaks.   25
O speak again, bright angel, for thou art
As glorious to this night, being o'er my head,
As is a winged messenger of heaven
Unto the white upturned, wond'ring eyes
Of mortals that fall back to gaze on him,   30
When he bestrides the lazy-passing clouds,
And sails upon the bosom of the air.
JULIET: O Romeo, Romeo, wherefore art thou Romeo?
Deny thy father, and refuse thy name.
Or if thou wilt not, be but sworn my love,   35
And I'll no longer be a Capulet.
ROMEO: [Aside] Shall I hear more, or shall I speak at this?
JULIET: 'Tis but thy name that is my enemy.
Thou art thyself, though not a Montague.
What's Montague? It is nor hand nor foot,   40
Nor arm nor face, nor any other part
Belonging to a man. O be some other name.
What's in a name? That which we call a rose
By any other word would smell as sweet.
So Romeo would, were he not Romeo called,   45
Retain that dear perfection which he owes

> Without that title. Romeo doff thy name,
> And for that name which is no part of thee,
> Take all myself.
> ROMEO: I take thee at thy word.
> Call me but 'love', and I'll be new baptized.   50
> Henceforth I never will be Romeo.
> JULIET: What man art thou, that thus be screened in night
> So stumblest on my counsel?
> ROMEO: By a name,
> I know not how to tell thee who I am.
> My name, dear saint, is hateful to myself,   55
> Because it is an enemy to thee.
> Had I it written, I would tear the word.
> JULIET: My ears have not yet drunk a hundred words
> Of thy tongue's uttering, yet I know the sound.
> Art thou not Romeo, and a Montague?   60
> ROMEO: Neither, fair maid, if either thee dislike.
> JULIET: How cam'st thou hither, tell me, and wherefore?

Romeo and Juliet have first met two scenes earlier at Capulet's feast (I. v. 90–107): before the Nurse called Juliet away, they spoke a sonnet and a quatrain together, touched hands and kissed. This is their second meeting, and now they can only talk.

Shakespeare shows each enter alone and remain in danger of discovery: Romeo may even risk death (see line 65) by having leapt over the orchard wall to be near Juliet. Although at the Globe Theatre this scene would be played in daylight, the two actors will move as if barely visible to each other in moonlight; at first Juliet is unaware of Romeo's presence, and when she does hear him she still cannot recognize his face. So their meeting is both secret and attended with abrupt disturbances:

> What man art thou that thus bescreened in night
> So stumblest on my counsel?   (52-3)

Later she speaks of the 'mask of night' and 'dark night' (85 and 106). Romeo suspects that

> Being in night, all this is but a dream,
> Too flattering-sweet to be substantial.   (140-1)

And all the time, Juliet is at a window, above the level of the platform stage where Romeo moves and stands. (This scene is traditionally called 'The Balcony Scene', but the text speaks only of a 'window', a far more confining structure.) The lovers cannot even touch each other; they meet and part several times within the single scene. To respond fully to the poetry of this passage, it is necessary to realize that the accompanying physical action is confined, quiet, alert, urgent, insecure and, at first, unco-ordinated.

The fact that the Globe audience could see both figures perfectly would make their searchings for each other seem the more strange and more obviously due to conditions not within their power. Yet it is not only night that delays recognitions: this is made abundantly clear, soon after their separate entries, by a silence that follows the short line 11. When Juliet speaks, 'she says nothing' (12), and, although Romeo says he will 'answer', he too must be silent for a moment as his intention changes:

> I am too bold, 'tis not to me she speaks. (14)

At the beginning of a long duet of words, Shakespeare shows both lovers speechless because they are unable to express their thoughts even to themselves: their desire to speak out is repressed by some kind of fear. Despite all the verbal felicities of this meet-ing, some of its most intense moments involve feelings beyond the reach of words. The 'darkness' and the separation of the figures are used to sharpen attention, and to ensure that the audience senses this salient fact. These lovers, although they never say as much, are prisoners without and within.

Shakespeare has also ensured that two individuals meet: their loves are mutual, but the quality of each is distinct. They use differing epithets, images and sentiments: Romeo speaks of lights and skies; Juliet of a 'rose' and 'dear perfection'. And a further expression of their complementary natures lies in the sound of the dialogue: each speaker has independent rhythms and impulses, and yet, at certain times, each responds sensitively to the other's rhythms. This musical element of the duet does much to achieve the impression of continuous excitement and mutual understanding at a deep level of consciousness – again an element that they cannot describe in words.

Romeo starts with a single, full line, responding to Mercutio's mockery in the previous scene and, as Juliet appears or moves behind the window, a verse-line is broken between 'But soft' and the longer response: 'what light through yonder window breaks?' Immediately the rhythm changes again in two lines that are broken after their fourth syllables, the second taking a greater weight of stress and sound. The third line (5) runs more lightly, with possibly a slight break after the sixth syllable and with scarcely a stop at its conclusion before the end of the sentence in a fourth line; this has two slight pauses after the second and fourth syllables, more back vowels with the warmer 'art far', together with alliteration and regular stress. Then a new sequence begins with an immediate counterstatement in a decisive four-syllable phrase; this is then elaborated more lightly until the end of the line, with a rhythm reminiscent of line 4 but without the firm stress at its end. The next line again starts with two main stresses in the regular iambic pattern, but this time there is no clear break, the line running on to 'sick and green' which gives a regular ending, but with consonants less smooth than previously. The conclusion to this second sequence of three lines is a regular pentameter divided after the seventh syllable, so that the final 'cast it off' has sharp and decisive energy; it is also abrupt in syntax. Romeo's verbal rhythm is thus clear: a quick energy, followed by a more sustained response. He tends to lengthen his phrasing in each sequence of thought and feeling; though, for the second main unit (lines 3–9), he concludes with an additional short phrase of three syllables only. Here is a lively pulse, a widening imaginative response, and unflagging energy.

When he sees Juliet more clearly, his excitement gives two almost equal exclamations within one iambic pentameter, followed, this time, with a further exclamation of only six syllables that leave a line incomplete. Now there is no following amplifying phrase. After the silence, the next line (12) is broken two times, again with an abrupt three-syllable conclusion. Line 13 is broken once. Line 14 returns to the earlier pattern of four-and-six, found in lines 3, 4, 6 and 7; and then longer rhythms are restored in a three-line sentence; but now the mid-line break tends to come after the sixth or fifth syllable, and there is the first clear run-on at the end of the second line (16). This arrangement of phrases within the iambic pattern gives a more sustained impulse, which is continued at the start of the following sentence (lines 18–20). The second line of this group may well have no break at all, and line 20 starts a new syntactical unit that runs into the following line without a break and is not completed until the fourth syllable of line 22. On this second encounter, phrases have again become progressively extended without loss of energy; the final sentence is elaborated to fill out the pentameter, with six syllables giving two consecutive stresses at the end. In much the same way Romeo's responses to Juliet's actions and utterance are expressed in two units, the first of three lines, the second of seven (lines 23–5 and 26–32).

Juliet's words have rhythms that are much less sustained, first simply 'Ay me', and then, after silence, an iambic broken twice (three-two-five) in which each new phrase begins with a stressed syllable. The next two lines (34 and 35) are broken after the fifth and sixth syllables. Only line 36 runs its full length, when she thinks of herself and not of Romeo; it is a strong conclusion, but achieved with only three strong stresses. Romeo then speaks a single line with his characteristic break after the fourth syllable, but, because it stands alone without his characteristic development, it also seems to be a response to her broken rhythms. In Juliet's next, longer speech (lines 38–49), broken lines again predominate, but now mostly in the four-six pattern. As in her previous utterance, simple words are echoed from phrase to phrase, giving a reiterative sound that accentuates the short pulse. Line 46 is the first that seems to call for a single phrase or, at least, sustains its first half until the seventh syllable: it is also the first line of Juliet's in which a noun is directly linked with a descriptive epithet in 'dear perfection', and the first in which sense runs on into the beginning of the following line. Probably the penultimate line (48) is without a break; but this has no epithet and, after a pause at the end, Juliet brings the whole speech to a conclusion strongly with four syllables of absolute committal, 'Take all myself', placed at head of the next line. The sentiment, the turning back of her thoughts upon herself, is like that at the end of her previous speech, 'And I'll no longer be a Capulet'; but it is strengthened, the shorter phrase carrying more weight, and remains in time with the quick-pulsed rhythm of her inner excitement.

The lovers now meet. First Romeo completes Juliet's verse-line, echoing her words in her own manner. Then he has three phrases of appeal and affirmation: the first two make one line (four-and-six) and the third extends to a full line by giving the three syllables of his own name clear articulation. Juliet's response lacks the firm rhythms of her earlier speeches in this scene; the second incomplete line (53) seems to run particularly lightly because it lacks the usual strong stress on the fourth syllable. Again Romeo completes her verse-line, but without the strength of his earlier interjection: here, 'By a name' (53) would have to be given two strong stresses if it were to complete the iambic penta-meter with assurance. His next line runs with simple mono-syllables. Only line 55, repeating 'name' and breaking the phrase by introducing 'dear saint' on the third and fourth syllables, shows anything like his earlier energy, until the concluding line (57) asserts a five-five pattern. The crux of the meeting is that 'dear saint' of line 55: it is a quotation from their first meeting (I. v. 100) that neither could fail to recognize, for it was the keystone of the word-play of their shared sonnet. Juliet's next words show that the phrase has sent her thoughts back to that moment, as Romeo's earlier talk had not done: it is the secret password, or charm, that opens the door to recognition and establishes the emotional intimacy again through words. Juliet's reply is no longer short-phrased; her first line runs over to the next line which, after a slight break on its fifth syllable, ends strongly and affirmatively. Then both speak with lighter rhythms, lines 61 and 62 being alive with short and simple phrases. If a member of an audience did not understand a word of English, he could appreciate the excitements, hesitations, assurances, answers and, finally, the shared and almost silent intimacy of this wooing in the very sound of the words that are spoken: the rhythms express emotion; they suggest physical activity and sexual involvement. If actors use these rhythms in their physical and vocal performances, they will recreate the inner excitement of the scene as Shakespeare conceived it.

Of course the words work directly too, in varying ways. Besides the broader contrasts between the visual images evoked by the two lovers, the general simplicity and repetition of Juliet's vocabulary are in contrast with the complexity of Romeo's.[1] His ornate words are offset at first only by his simpler responses to Juliet's action of resting her face in her hand, and to her words; yet, when he calls on his 'dear saint', he is, for the moment, as simple in vocabulary as Juliet.

The interchanges of vocabulary are subtle: for example after the intimate recognition, Romeo expostulates, saying he would 'tear' his written name, and this physical verb seems to draw forth the equally physical 'drunk' in Juliet's reply. Both speakers use images of war and conflict. Romeo's first words are of 'scars' and 'wounds', and the light is said to 'break' through the window, like daybreak; this leads quickly to 'kill the envious moon'. But the more he sees and hears of Juliet, the less conflict is reflected in his speech, the only traces being 'bold', 'shamed' and 'fall back'. Juliet, in contrast, speaks first of 'Deny', 'refuse' and 'sworn', and only then, directly and unambiguously, of 'enemy'; but she carefully dissociates this from Romeo, applying it specifically to his name. After their mutual recognition Romeo also uses 'enemy'.

The words of both speakers also give sexual definition to the encounter. Levitation and flight are often expressive of sexual excitement in dreams and fantasies, and this element in Romeo's

[1] Later, in the scene at Friar Lawrence's cell before their marriage, Juliet's imagery is as confident and sustained as Romeo's, perhaps more steadily so; see II. vi. 24-34.

imagery is continuously developed, from a rising sun, to stars streaming through the 'airy region', to a 'winged messenger' riding on the clouds and sailing on 'the bosom of the air'; with this last image Romeo sees himself as a mortal who falls back to gaze at the 'bright angel' that passes over during the night. Juliet tries, with increasing ingenuity, to separate Romeo from his name, distinguishing first a hand, foot, arm and face, and then 'any other part belonging to a man'. Thinking in this way of his body, her next thought is of a 'rose', symbol of beauty, perfection, passion and attraction; then she considers Romeo's 'dear perfection', a phrase at once unspecific, intense and delicately all-embracing.

Perhaps the most extraordinary quality in this passage is its secret necessity. Neither character speaks directly of this, but both are drawn together, physically, rhythmically, verbally and sexually. As Juliet responds silently to 'dear saint', Romeo seems to know as much, and he gathers new energy for his concluding line, an energy to which Juliet, in her turn, instinctively responds. In the last line quoted here, Juliet's questions show curiosity and fear following quickly on that complete acceptance of Romeo's presence which Juliet has not verbally communicated – it has been an acknowledged inner necessity.

Act IV, Scene i

JULIET: O bid me leap, rather than marry Paris,   77
    From off the battlements of any tower;
    Or walk in thievish ways; or bid me lurk
    Where serpents are; chain me with roaring bears;   80
    Or hide me nightly in a charnel-house,
    O'er-covered quite with dead men's rattling bones,
    With reeky shanks and yellow chapless skulls;
    Or bid me go into a new-made grave,
    And hide me with a dead man in his shroud;   85
    – Things that to hear them told have made me tremble –
    And I will do it without fear or doubt,
    To live an unstained wife to my sweet love.

The reading of line 85 is from the unauthoritative fourth Quarto edition of 1622. The first, 'bad' Quarto read 'Or lay me in a tomb with one new dead', and the 'good' Quarto (which is the most reliable text) read the line as printed above but with no word at all after 'his'. For this obvious omission, the Folio edition of 1623 supplied 'grave' – which is not a convincing reading since the same word concludes the previous line. Obviously Q2 represents an improvement over the earlier reading as a whole, and an editor needs only to supply some monosyllabic noun at the end, 'shroud' being very suitable. If it be objected, as by Terence Spencer, the New Penguin editor, 'that it would be difficult to hide in the *shroud* already occupied by a dead man', we may answer that practicality has little to do with an excited and strained fantasy, and may accept the possible absurdity instead of adopting 'tomb' from Q1 as does Professor Spencer. Certainly in IV. iii Juliet, again envisioning death, imagines that she will

> . . . Madly play with my forefathers' joints,
> And pluck the mangled Tybalt from his shroud.
>
> (51–2)

The word is not foreign to the context.

The most notable feature of the whole speech is its teeming and cumulative imagery. The progression is significant, showing how the speaker's mind responds ever more fully. First the daring 'leap' from the battlements, suggesting warfare and imprisonment; then the more sustained 'walk' along paths of suspicion and danger; then waiting nowhere specific in the creeping and sinister presence of poisonous snakes. All these phrases are linked with the verb 'bid' (lines 77 and 79), implying that Juliet has to perform the functions for herself; but then she thinks of herself as a victim being 'chained' with 'roaring bears', in a pit where she will be at the mercy of onlookers. From this she thinks of being 'hidden' in a 'charnel house' where bones from old burials are stored; now it is night-time and she is overwhelmed with the scattered bones and with noise. Her senses are awakening to the horror, so that with the macabre sound of the bones, she realizes in her imagination the smell and colour of decomposing legs and heads. In language she is now more homely, speaking of 'shanks' and 'chaps' (or lower jaws), as if drawn onwards to realize the remains of bodies without dignity or nicety, though with particular detail. In this overwhelming and active place of horror, she again imagines herself being bidden (84) to act. This time a single possibility is realized in two stages, the first comparatively simple – entering a 'new-made grave' – and the second precise, but intimate and physical in its imagined action: it must involve her instinctive and total response to a 'dead man'.

The terminus of this chain of images is more than a contact with death; it is also an echo of almost the last words she had spoken to Romeo:

> O God, I have an ill-divining soul.
> Methinks I see thee now thou art so low,
> As one dead in the bottom of a tomb.
> Either my eyesight fails, or thou lookest pale.
>
> (III. v. 54–7)

There is, moreover, a series of sexual allusions in her visions of death that grow in power. They start in the flying 'leap' and the creeping 'serpents'; and they probably continue through the animality of 'bears' and the secrecy of 'nightly'. In the two 'hide's', and in 'o'er-covered' and 'shanks', she is close to imagining herself pressed upon by men's bodies. She finishes 'hidden' with a 'dead man'—with Romeo.

Line 85 is, then, a climax in several ways. It is not the most sustained image – the previous one runs to three lines – but it is introduced with two verbs, 'bid' and 'hide'. All the preceding lines could take a slight break in mid-line; but lines 84 and 85 seem to call for continuous phrasing. The first of them, like several others, has only four stresses, giving a light middle foot so that emphasis accrues for 'new-made grave' at the end of the line. Then the second and climactic line, exceptionally in this passage, is without a clear stress on its fourth syllable, the position in an iambic pentameter which can least easily suffer irregularity; moreover the fourth foot has a reversed stress so that both 'dead' and 'man' take emphasis and thus prepare for a further impression of resolution on 'shroud' at the end of the line. It will sound as if the speaker finds this last image hard to sustain, and yet just succeeds, perhaps with forced rhythm.

After this line (85) there is a change of involvement. The sequence of images breaks off for a descriptive parenthesis. Why is this? Juliet suddenly thinks of herself, becomes self-conscious even; there is probably a clear physical change, and almost certainly she should be trembling, as her words suggest. The speech had started as an assurance to Friar Lawrence that she will 'undertake A thing like death' (73-4) to avoid a second marriage; the brief 'rather than marry Paris' (77) shows that her mind is at first quite conscious of this persuasive purpose. But as the images develop, she is concerned only with realizing what the deed might be like. If line 86 is spoken for Friar Lawrence's sake, it would sound like an excuse for her terrified reaction and also a vow to actually meet such horrors, to withstand and surpass the worst of imagined horrors. But the line could also be a correction of balance, an involuntary self-awareness to mark for herself this progress towards facing her destiny. Certainly she now vows simply and directly, for the next line seems calm, with a thoughtful stress coming on the fourth syllable: 'And I will *do* it . . .' In this speech there is an emotional and physical performance that must startle as much by its assured return to deliberation as in its wild, cumulative and hardly controlled involvement with fantasies of danger, fear and sex.

With the doublet 'fear and doubt' the expression of Juliet's resolution is shown to be carefully measured, the second element implying suspicion and distrust. The concluding line has thoughtful stress on 'un-' and 'my' dictated by the iambics; a straight and bold assertion of domesticity in 'wife', a title so recently and dearly claimed by Juliet; and a direct and unforced expression of affection in 'sweet love'. The metre is steadily and fully followed by the words. Only the choice of 'un*stained*' and the affirmative, yet again simple, 'live', reflect backwards on the macabre and hallucinatory images of the first nine lines. In the dramatic context,

c

it is moving and pathetic to hear and see Juliet thus collected, in command and yet so gently in command. The Friar's next line has a brisk satisfaction:

> Hold then, go home, be merry, give consent
> To marry Paris . . .   (89–90)

but there is a disproportion in Juliet's speech which must surely make the audience more uneasy of the outcome than the Friar's words imply. There are huge forces within Juliet's own imagination that she will have to confront without her counsellor's help.

The emotional, physical and sexual pressures *implied* by the images and rhythms of lines 77–85 are the very basis of this speech in performance – the secret actuality within an artificial catalogue of horrors. The control of mood within such short compass in the last three lines provides further dramatic excitement, anticipation and ironies: Juliet achieves a perilous moment of assurance which she cannot truly evaluate; the audience may sense her true predicament, but it may well not. Shakespeare has presented this emotional crux of the drama in a delicate and open manner.

Act V, Scene iii

ROMEO: In faith I will. Let me peruse this face.
   Mercutio's kinsman, noble County Paris!   75
   What said my man, when my betossed soul
   Did not attend him as we rode? I think
   He told me Paris should have married Juliet.
   Said he not so? Or did I dream it so?
   Or am I mad, hearing him talk of Juliet,   80
   To think it was so? O give me thy hand,
   One writ with me in sour misfortune's book.
   I'll bury thee in a triumphant grave.
   A grave? O no, a lantern, slaughtered youth;
   For here lies Juliet, and her beauty makes   85
   This vault a feasting presence full of light.

Death, lie thou there, by a dead man interred.
How oft when men are at the point of death
Have they been merry, which their keepers call
A lightning before death. O how may I   90
Call this a lightning? O my love, my wife!
Death that hath sucked the honey of thy breath,
Hath had no power yet upon thy beauty.
Thou art not conquered; beauty's ensign yet
Is crimson in thy lips and in thy cheeks,   95
And death's pale flag is not advanced there.
Tybalt, liest thou there in thy bloody sheet?
O what more favour can I do to thee,
Than with that hand that cut thy youth in twain
To sunder his that was thine enemy?   100
Forgive me cousin. Ah dear Juliet,
Why art thou yet so fair? Shall I believe
That unsubstantial death is amorous,
And that the lean abhorred monster keeps
Thee here in dark to be his paramour?   105
For fear of that, I still will stay with thee,
And never from this palace of dim night
Depart again. Here, here will I remain
With worms that are thy chamber-maids. O here
Will I set up my everlasting rest;   110
And shake the yoke of inauspicious stars
From this world-wearied flesh. Eyes look your last.
Arms, take your last embrace. And lips, O you
The doors of breath, seal with a righteous kiss
A dateless bargain to engrossing death.   115
[*Takes out the poison*] Come bitter conduct, come unsavoury
   guide,
Thou desperate pilot, now at once run on
The dashing rocks thy sea-sick weary bark.
Here's to my love [*Drinks*] O true apothecary!
Thy drugs are quick. Thus with a kiss I die.   120

This final soliloquy of Romeo's is not the usual sort in which a
character steps forward to deliberate or to disclose previously
hidden sentiments; only in the sense that Romeo thinks he is the

one living person on stage is this a solo speech. He addresses many people as well as himself: the dead Paris and Tybalt, and the seemingly dead Juliet; he apostrophizes his own eyes, arms and lips, the poison and the apothecary who sold it. Speech fulfils many functions: he questions, comments, describes, directs, vows, states, calls and exclaims. A continuous energy of thought and feeling directs his words to a wide variety of purposes within a short time.

Nor is this energy wholly in words. There are many physical activities, growing ever more numerous and important towards the end. He 'peruses' (74) the face of the man he killed; he takes his 'hand' (81) and probably drags him across the floor until he is suitably 'interred' (87). He looks at Juliet while he is doing this and again immediately afterwards (see lines 85 and 91–6); he then looks at the dead Tybalt and back again to Juliet (see lines 97 and 101). At this point he is particularly conscious of his surroundings, the Capulet funeral vault (see lines 105, 108 and 109), and then he lifts up the apparently dead body of Juliet to embrace and kiss her. Although these last actions are clearly described in lines 112–115, it is just possible that he does not perform them until after he has taken the poison (line 120); but at least he must be about to enact what he describes at this point, and then break off to kill himself. At line 116 he takes out the poison, pours it into some cup (see line 161 below) and drinks it. At once he must feel great pain, for he exclaims immediately that the 'drugs are quick' (120) and then, overcoming pain, he kisses Juliet and dies. Later in the scene he is found lying across her 'bosom' (line 155, below), so probably he dies kissing her a second time, and not in a continuation of the 'last embrace' he had called for at line 113; or else he is prevented a second time from the embrace he had called for. Either way, his last movements must be urgent as well as loving, as brief as the words which are their accompaniment.

The rhythms of speech, as represented by versification and syntax, well suggest a growing pressure of activity. The iambic pentameters, as usually in this play, run fully and regularly. At the beginning, after the fight with Paris, the lines are almost all broken by necessary punctuation or some slight pause. But when

he begins to consider his fate more deeply there are several unbroken lines; see especially line 86, which has run over from the
previous line, and 88, running over to 89; and then, in fairly quick
succession, lines 92, 93, 96 and 98. Lines 104, 105 and 107 may each
run their full length without a break, and again 110 and 111. But
the concluding lines are all broken, with shorter rhythms; and now
simple words and phrases are repeated immediately and so help to
give Romeo's last utterance insistence and tense strength. Line
113 is broken three times, after the first, sixth and eighth syllables;
only line 115 could run its full length in a single phrase. The choice
and order of words in lines 117 and 118 require more than the one
break that is marked in this text by a comma after 'pilot': slight
pauses after 'now' and 'once', 'rocks' and 'sea-sick' or 'weary'
also seem necessary in order to give sufficient control and clarity.
There is no doubt at all that the last two lines, instead of coming
to a full close in the rhyming couplet or firmly regular iambic
pentameter which are normal for the soliloquies and longer
speeches in this play, need firm breaks after each fourth syllable,
and must be accompanied by action that makes large demands on
the actor. Increasingly the soliloquy requires strenuous and absorbing physical involvement, and more and more rapid alter-
nations of feeling, thought and purpose; and all this is marked, and
indeed controlled and supported, by the phrasing of speech,
metre and rhythms.

One remarkable feature of the vocabulary reinforces this active
impression: the choice of verbs. They are almost all of utmost
simplicity, and mostly monosyllabic and Anglo-Saxon in origin.
The exceptions are 'peruse', 'attend' and 'interred' near the
beginning, and a small group of military activities appropriate to
the extended image of lines 94–100: 'conquered', 'advanced' and
'sunder'. For the rest, Romeo's engagement with death is indicated with athletic assurance and economy: will, let, said, rode,
think, told, married, said, dream, am, hearing, think, was, give,
writ, bury, lies, makes, lie, are, been, call (twice), sucked, had, is,
liest, can, do, cut, was, forgive, art, believe, is, keeps, be, stay,
depart, remain, are, set, shake, look, take, seal, come (twice),

run, is, are, die. Romeo does not attain a philosophic state of mind that needs complicated or sophisticated verbs to express it: his grasp remains simple and strong. (Compare, for example, some of the verbs in Hamlet's much shorter last speech: o'ercrows, prophesy, lights, solicited.) Romeo's death is remarkable for the sharp conjuncture and interaction of many basically uncomplicated verbal elements.

As elsewhere in this play, metaphors and images extend the reference and allusiveness of speech. Some, in the usual manner, grow in strength, starting from a brief word and being developed to a full line, or seeming to grow out of an earlier related image. So 'lantern' of line 84 leads to the 'feasting presence full of light' of line 86; and 'light' leads on to 'lightning' of lines 90 and 91. The unremarkable 'power' of line 93 starts a sequence of military terms extending to line 100. But with these few developing images are others, no less suggestive, that live only fitfully: 'be-tossed soul', early in line 76 seems to leave no trace on the rest of the speech, unless the associations surface again in 'sea-sick, weary bark', three lines before the end; 'one writ with me in sour misfortune's book' (82) and 'sucked the honey of thy breath' (92) also seem to die at once, re-emerging, perhaps, much later in 'seal with a righteous kiss a dateless bargain . . .' (114-15) and 'doors of breath' (114). Towards the end, 'feasting presence' returns as 'palace of dim night' and is developed, briefly and macabrely, with 'worms that are thy chamber-maids' (107 and 109). The soliloquy ends, however, with three once-and-for-all images – 'rest', 'yoke', and 'seal' – that are rejected as soon as uttered. There is one remarkable series that does finally extend to a full-line phrase, but it grows in strength only with contradictory epithets that deny free scope to its associations: '*bitter* conduct . . . *unsavoury* guide . . . *desperate* pilot'; and with 'dashing rocks' and '*sea-sick, weary* bark' of line 118, the image of sea travel is accompanied with epithets which are so restlessly full of suggestion that they half obscure the basic metaphor-picture.

Puns still further sharpen and complicate the end of the soliloquy. The first, on lightning/lightening (of spirits) is deliberately presented in successive lines (90–1), but 'favour' (good turn/mark of honour) is only a possibility that may or may not be marked. In the last lines, puns are more frequent, quite brief and quite inescapable. 'Everlasting rest' refers to a stake 'set up' for betting *and* to the 'rest' of death, *and* (in view of 'paramour' of line 105 and the identical pun at IV. v. 6) to sexual satisfaction; 'shake' of the next line may add another betting pun. In line 115, 'dateless' means endless *and* always valid, while 'engrossing' means 'accounting' *and* 'monopolizing', *and*, possibly, with a backward glance to 'unsubstantial' and 'lean' of lines 103–4, fattening or well fed. In the final two lines the puns are both simpler and more far-reaching: 'true' is 'promising truly' and also 'true to his calling in curing Romeo's ills'; 'quick' is 'speedy', *and* 'alive' or, even, 'life-giving'. The last word of all, 'die', in association with the life-giving 'kiss', may perhaps have some echo of its Elizabethan usage, meaning 'to have sexual satisfaction'. Such word-play suggests heightened, tense and restless self-consciousness.

A further step is necessary to understand what happens on the stage as the last six, simple-seeming words are spoken. The meanings and associations of words and the expressiveness of rhythms, gestures and physical activity all concur, with their growing vitality, to give an impression of a man's mind and being which is actuated at a depth of consciousness below that capable of direct expression in words or deeds. It is, indeed, the ruthless pressures of the last few lines that give the crowning impression of Romeo's sensitivity – the secret, unspoken valour, and the commanding awareness of himself and others.

Imagine an actor of Romeo who asks throughout the soliloquy, 'why do I say or do this?' Some movements from phrase to phrase will be easy to understand, others puzzling; some will seem to represent a development of an emotional, intellectual or physical activity, and others simply a large, and perhaps surprising or shocking, change of involvement – a transition, as eighteenth-century actors commonly termed such an opportunity for impressive acting. In this soliloquy Romeo's attention is carried away from himself to his surroundings, to Juliet, to preparation for death, and back to himself; and each movement is made five or six times within the forty-six lines. With these variations in the object or cause of thought and feeling, his mood and response is continually changing too: activity; recollection; awareness that he may be asleep or mad (79–80); active sympathy; wonder; self-dramatizing irony; merriness (89); surprise, wonder, tenderness and renewed wonder (90–5); sympathy and self-questioning (96–101); wonder, doubt and 'fear' (or jealousy); avowal ... Towards the end of the soliloquy, self-awareness and out-going avowal became constant, but varied with passing strains of tenderness, weariness, haste, insistence, resistance to pain and, at last, a simple physical affirmation that lacks an answer.

In the last lines there are echoes which suggest that Romeo is also remembering earlier experiences and so setting a seal upon them. In a previous scene the apothecary had claimed that his drugs were 'quick' (see V. i. 77–9), and Romeo had described him as lean and wretched (like a figure of Death), a seller of 'cordial' to the 'life-weary taker' (V. i. 85 and 62). More significantly still, the image of the pilot (see lines 116–18) echoes several of Romeo's earlier speeches. Before going to Capulet's feast his mind had feared 'some consequence, yet hanging in the stars';

> But he that hath the steerage of my course
> Direct my suit. On lusty gentlemen.   (I. iv. 106–13)

When he had been welcomed by Juliet under her window, he vowed:

> I am no pilot, yet wert thou as far
> As that vast shore washed with the farthest sea,
> I should adventure for such merchandise.   (II. ii. 82–4)

After he had refused to fight with Juliet's cousin Tybalt, and Tybalt had slain Mercutio, he vowed that 'fire-eyed fury' should be his 'conduct now' (III. i. 120). Any or all of these moments may echo in the audience's mind during the last lines of the soliloquy but, even if they do not, they will certainly give to the actor a reference back by which he will clarify his present engagement in the drama and give his speech steadiness and assurance. In any one performance the effect may be slight, but however achieved, it can only serve to sharpen, secretly, the impression of Romeo's striving and controlled consciousness.

The most noticeable impressions of Romeo's unspoken motivation will come from those transitions which depend on non-verbal means, and those which most surprisingly juxtapose reactions that are normally antagonistic. First, the sudden self-consciousness of 'Let me peruse this face' expresses an otherwise unstated need to control his awareness of his situation. Then the transition from self-awareness to 'O give me thy hand' (81) expresses a sense of kinship with the dead enemy that is not verbally clarified until the next line. In line 84, the transition from considering the grave to a response to Juliet's beauty is clearly motivated by the sight of her, but again the explanation follows the reaction and thus Romeo again seems drawn instinctively. With 'Death, lie thou there, by a dead man interred' (87), self-awareness has returned but interpenetrated with a recognition that death is near, indeed already present; and this springs, paradoxically, from 'feasting presence full of light', a warm and rich image of Juliet's beauty: – Romeo is drawn by love and death, despair and hope, almost in one moment. Rhythm, word-order, the return of self-consciousness will here help the actor to reveal the collision of responses, and how Romeo's fatalism is instinctive and alive within his keenest response to Juliet. The next transition to a kind of merriment will seem like a nervous escape; but this route leads only deeper, to a question sharpened by a pun: 'O how may I call this a lightning?' The simplest words in the whole soliloquy follow, 'O my love, my wife!' (91): this implies another huge transition, this time to simple affection rather than wonder; and it has been effected by the sight and presence of Juliet in the tomb. Few or none of the audience could explain what has happened or be conscious of the effective source of dramatic excitement, but the inward and physical changes, the shifts and relaxations of tensions within the actor which are neces-sary to allow him to speak these contrasting exclamations, will make themselves clear visually and rhythmically in his stage presence, and in the speaking of 'O my love, my wife'. The bare words in such a position will seem alive with tenderness and resolve; they are transformed from simplicity to subtlety because they carry the powerful, inarticulate transition.

Romeo now controls his response in an extended martial image, and from this moves easily enough to remember Tybalt. Then he is again conscious of Juliet. The transition is made, this second time, with less sudden urgency, but it leads at once to questions and to a conscious rivalry with death. The sense of loss develops by firm stages to a fantasy of Juliet as Death's paramour, and it is this which precipitates Romeo's vow to die with Juliet, as he had intended when he came to the tomb. He becomes aware, again, of his surroundings, and thoughts of death lead to his last resolutions. From now on there is no surprising transition; rather a steady development of a single determination, as he concludes his life and suffering. The imagery is varied; speech is sharpened by puns and echoes, and broken for purposeful actions, the acceptance of pain and the experiencing of joy and love. Romeo is absorbed in what he must do, and yet self-aware and able to remember the apothecary; and in all this variety of feeling and consciousness there is an undeflected intention that leads and develops steadily. The conscious being that the audience now senses beneath the words and actions, the impression of character which is their unifying cause and inner reality, has, at last, an achieved strength and a liberty or openness of mind. It is this which is the main dramatic surprise and achievement of this scene, not the association of death and love, which has been foretold many times, from the phrase 'death-marked love' of the Prologue onwards.

The audience is not wholly involved in Romeo's consciousness, for it may remember at any time that Juliet is alive and that Romeo's death will be mocked by her reawakening. Twice his words unmistakably remind his hearers of this, despite his own ignorance: 'Death ... Hath had no power yet upon thy beauty' (92–3) and 'Why art thou yet so fair ...?' (101–5). When he cries 'Here's to my love' (119) and drinks poison, he echoes

Juliet's 'Romeo! Romeo! Romeo! I drink to thee,' as she had taken the potion that had made her lie as if dead (IV. iii. 58). These visual and verbal echoes at the latest moment may remind the audience of Romeo's true situation, so that they know, as he does not, that chance, luck or fate governs his death, together with his own resolution. For all the intense interest that must be aroused for Romeo's inward thoughts and feelings, the audience will be half-aware, at least from time to time, that he is deceived, and that his death, in itself, is pointless. It is this view that is carried forward in the busy entry of Friar Lawrence that immediately follows. He carries a light and 'crow and spade', as Romeo had done, but, ineffectually, he prays aloud 'Saint Francis be my speed' (V. iii. 121). At this point, if not before, the audience must see and hear the helplessness of these urgent figures.

This passage, like the previous one, shows how Shakespeare gives the audience an opportunity to take a deeper and wider view of a character's involvement than the words explicitly suggest; to respond to the drama is both a discovery and an encounter, controlled and essentially free.

Act V, Scene iii

PRINCE: This letter doth make good the friar's words,   285
    Their course of love, the tidings of her death.
    And here he writes that he did buy a poison
    Of a poor pothecary, and therewithal
    Came to this vault to die and lie with Juliet.
    Where be these enemies? Capulet, Montague,   290
    See what a scourge is laid upon your hate,
    That heaven finds means to kill your joys with love.
    And I for winking at your discords too
    Have lost a brace of kinsmen; all are punished.
CAPULET: O brother Montague, give me thy hand.   295
    This is my daughter's jointure, for no more
    Can I demand.
MONTAGUE: But I can give thee more.
    For I will raise her statue in pure gold,

That whiles Verona by that name is known,
There shall no figure at such rate be set   300
As that of true and faithful Juliet.
CAPULET: As rich shall Romeo by his lady lie,
Poor sacrifices of our enmity.
PRINCE: A glooming peace this morning with it brings;
The sun for sorrow will not show his head.   305
Go hence to have more talk of these sad things;
Some shall be pardoned, and some punished.
For never was a story of more woe
Than this of Juliet and her Romeo.

Exeunt

The concluding words of this tragedy are immediately intelligible;
the syntax is straightforward, and versification, except for rhymes,
unremarkable. The sequence of thought and feeling involves
no sudden transitions nor subtextual cross-currents. Discounting
proper names, the number of polysyllables is unusually low and,
with the single exception of 'glooming' (304), epithets are as
obvious as black and white: good, poor, pure, no, such, true,
faithful, rich, poor, more, sad, more. Yet, in performance, the
end of a tragedy must hold attention and carry the accumulated
interest of the audience with some kind of strengthened satisfaction until the last moment.

To understand how this passage works in a theatre and to appreciate the need for the simplest possible words, the full stage-
picture must be envisaged in the mind's eye or, rather, the mind's
theatre. While only three people speak, the stage is crowded with
others all directly and intimately concerned with the catastrophe.
At the centre must stand the Prince, who has calmed the 'outcry'
(192) in and around the tomb, and now acts as judge. Also at the
centre must be the dead bodies of Romeo and Juliet, and near by
those of Tybalt still in a 'bloody sheet' (97) and Paris newly slain
with a sword. There are bloodstains on the floor, and 'masterless
and gory swords' that 'lie discoloured by this place of peace'
(140-3). Torches and lanterns probably light the stage (see line
170); and in Elizabethan public theatres they would probably

give an impression of actuality, for although performances were in the open air, the London season was mostly during winter months when the stage would darken towards the end of a play. Certainly all doors are closed and guarded as the Prince has earlier commanded:

> Seal up the mouth of outrage for a while,
> Till we can clear these ambiguities,
> And know their spring, their head, their true descent;
> And then will I be general of your woes,
> And lead you even to death. Meantime forbear,
> And let mischance be slave to patience.
> Bring forth the parties of suspicion. (215-21)

On stage around the central figures are the watchmen, with Friar Lawrence and Romeo's man, Balthasar, as their prisoners; and only a few moments before, they had said that the Friar 'trembles, sighs, and weeps' (183). Positioning themselves as far from each other as possible are the Capulets, headed by Capulet himself and Lady Capulet, and the Montagues, with the marked absence of Lady Montague who has died during the night. In addition there is Paris's page, and a sufficient number of attendants to protect and support the Prince and to guard the door.

The Prince's 'This letter doth make good the friar's words', must come after a silence in which he has read the letter. Already, during the spoken evidence of the 'parties of suspicion', there has been a remarkable silence: neither Capulet nor Montague had spoken, in exclamation or question, during the Friar's long account of secret marriage, feigned death, fatal accident of a letter undelivered, and fatal fear which had led him to leave Juliet alone in the tomb, all of which were revelations that involved them deeply. The Prince had conducted proceedings as briefly as possible, sparing only one line to reassure the Friar that his reputation had been that of a 'holy man' (269). The reason for such prolonged and unexpected silence was clearly grief, a grief that has specifically caused Lady Capulet and Montague to think of their own deaths (see lines 205-6 and 213-14). The new pause after the Page has given the last piece of verbal evidence, and before the Prince reveals the contents of the letter, is sustained by this general and accumulated tendency towards silence that has gone before, as much as by waiting for further information: it is, in effect, a moment when the audience recognizes and, probably, shares a corporate acceptance of helplessness and ignorance in the face of catastrophe.

The first five lines start with a demonstrative reference to the actual letter and, perhaps, an ironic pun as 'make good' is used of the ill news. Syntactically the lines move in parallel phrases, and there is a further reference to the actual letter in 'here' (287) together with a recognition of 'this vault' (289). The Prince seems to speak as objectively as possible, one point at a time; but the opposition of 'love' and 'death' in the second line is repeated in 'die' and 'lie' (289) where it is sharpened by the internal rhyme, the close similarity in weight between the two words, and the ambiguity of 'lying' in bed and lying in a grave, and of 'dying' in love and out of life (see p. 61 above). At this point there is a transition, perhaps after another brief silence, from the discovery of facts to the consequences of them; it is abrupt and simple:

> Where be these enemies? Capulet, Montague . . .

Then the Prince turns from human agency to impersonal force – loss and grief is called a 'scourge' that is 'laid' upon their hate – and then acknowledges supernatural influence. Again love and death come together, but turning this time on the transitive 'kill' rather than the intransitive 'die': 'heaven finds means to kill your joys with love'. Here, too, is another pun, for 'joys' means both children and happiness; and 'love' cannot bear an easy meaning, referring both to the affection of the lovers and to the parents' feelings for their children.

At this moment the focus of attention must be fixed on the culpable parents, in sharp awareness of their part in the catastrophe. In most productions the fathers kneel in submission, as the 'parties of suspicion' had done before them. It is, however, the Prince that speaks next, and this is perhaps Shakespeare's largest surprise and most original stroke in the whole concluding episode.

The centre of the silent tableau gives way; the judge judges himself:

> And I for winking at your discords too
> Have lost a brace of kinsmen; all are punished.

Trial scenes and royal judgements are common at the end of Elizabethan and Jacobean plays – indeed in plays of all ages – but I cannot recall one from this time in which the judge, having heard evidence and pronounced judgement, proceeds, unprompted, to implicate himself. Verona's Prince must show his sorrow and his complicity, as the prisoners and the parents have done before him.

From this common acknowledgement, the play moves forward again as Capulet speaks, breaking a silence of more than ninety lines: for the first time he calls Montague 'brother', and they take each other's hands. Their speeches are concerned with acknowledging the marriage, the worth, and the love and death of their children; the Prince's description of them as 'enemies' (290) is accepted in 'enmity' (303), his 'die and lie' echoed in 'lie' and 'sacrifices' (302–3); and Capulet introduces a new paradox between the 'rich' statues and the 'poor' (or grievous, helpless and, now, valueless) sacrifices of which they are to be the memorial. The commercial details of their talk are extended so that the audience may be aware that they hope to find common purpose at last in constructing lifeless reproductions of their children that will blatantly demonstrate wealth, purity, parity of regard and, above all, loss.

The spectacle of Capulet and Montague reconciled before the dead bodies of their children speaks without words of a new organization within the city of Verona, and fulfils the predictions of the play's Prologue. The Prince then reassumes the central position, and accepts 'peace' after emnity. The epithet 'glooming' which he attaches to their reconciliation is not used elsewhere by Shakespeare and, as we have already noted, it is the one wholly distinctive word in these last speeches. Previously Shakespeare had used 'gloomy' in 1 Henry VI:

> . . . darkness and the gloomy shade of death
> Environ you, till mischief and despair
> Drive you to break your necks or hang yourselves!
>
> (V. iv. 89–91)

and in *Titus Andronicus*:

> . . . wert thou thus surpriz'd, sweet girl,
> Ravished and wrong'd as Philomela was,
> Forc'd in the ruthless, vast, and gloomy woods? (IV. i 52–4)

The Prince speaks of peace as if it were dark and threatening, close to death and despair. He mentions, directly, 'sorrow', 'sad things' and 'woe'; and he brings the play to an end with a repetition of the names of Juliet and Romeo, speaking of them as agents in a completed story that has touched those who shared it as no other has done.

Another word introduced in the Prince's concluding speech is 'pardoned', which is linked with the 'punished' repeated from the last statement of his previous speech. No one responds verbally, but the audience may well note the word. There is ample time for such reflections as the people on stage 'Go hence', with the rival houses walking side by side and, presumably, following their Prince. Compare this with the end of other tragedies by Shakespeare: the military acclamation of *Hamlet*, the hopeful acknowledgement of grace and unity of *Macbeth*, the bearing away of the bodies in *King Lear* and the hiding of them behind bed-curtains in *Othello*. For *Romeo and Juliet* the bodies are left on stage – those of Tybalt and Paris as well as the lovers – and the stage must empty slowly as some twenty persons, many waiting for 'pardon' or 'punishment' make their exit; they leave a silence behind them and take away another within them.

When words are used in these last moments they have direct clarity, even in the few puns and allusive references that they possess. Speech is a painful rejection of silence: and the corporate and individual silences of living people among the dead, with implications of acknowledged responsibility and fellow-feeling, make the most inescapable impression. Only the Prince in speaking of 'heaven' (292) and the 'sun' (305) acknowledges, however slightly, some influence on events besides the characters' own culpability. But even his last words foresee only human activity, and acknowledge that the story was of 'Juliet and *her* Romeo'. In the context that simple personal pronoun, unstressed by metre or rhyme, can set the whole play reverberating in the minds of an audience: desire, possession, loss, individuality, responsibility and the fallibility and helplessness of human action.

The verbal simplicity and the large and often silent stage-picture act as sounding-boards for the expression of thought and feeling on stage, and for its communication to the audience; the very air seems alive with human suffering and desire. Shakespeare has developed this strangely affecting simplicity throughout this concluding episode with consummate theatrical art.

2 As You Like It

THE NEXT three plays to be considered were all written at the turn of the century, between 1599 and 1601 or 1602, and present contrasting moods: *As You Like It* ends with a dance and teasing epilogue, *Julius Caesar* with suicides and military victory, *Twelfth Night* with a procession and a cynical and melancholy song sung by a fool alone on the stage. Here, at midway in his career, the variety of Shakespeare's style is splendidly evident.

In *As You Like It*, the action moves from a country house and a Duke's court to the Forest of Arden, where sophisticated men and women confront shepherds, dress up as foresters, struggle (off stage) with wild animals, sing, talk and go to sleep. Incidents include disguise of sex, the appearance of the god Hymen, and, as Jaques walks away before the conclusion, a refusal to 'look at happiness through another man's eyes'. Energy of invention seems unending, and this is to be observed as much within single scenes as from scene to scene.

The extracts chosen for analysis are not the soliloquies or solo speeches, like Jaques on the Seven Ages of Man or the banished Duke on the pleasures of philosophizing, but corporate scenes. In the first, entries, exits and other movements across the stage are frequent and surprising, eloquent in themselves like the interplay of themes in music. In the second extract, shared and private thoughts are evoked and contrasted within a single duologue. In all, incidental variety is related to a consistent dramatic development, and between each scene unifying elements can be seen shaping the play as a whole. In considering the entry of Hymen and his train, in the last extract, it will be necessary to relate his song to all the others, for its effect depends on other moments when spoken dialogue gives way to musical utterance and individual reaction to group response.

Act I, Scene ii

DUKE FREDERICK: No more, no more.
ORLANDO: Yes I beseech your Grace,
   I am not yet well breathed.
DUKE FREDERICK: How dost thou Charles?
LE BEAU: He cannot speak my lord.
DUKE FREDERICK: Bear him away.   190
   What is thy name, young man?
ORLANDO: Orlando my liege,
   The youngest son of Sir Rowland de Boys.
DUKE FREDERICK: I would thou hadst been son to some man else.

By the usual literary standards these six lines would not be rated among Shakespeare's best; if encountered out of context they might not even be recognized as Shakespeare's. Even the versification seems hesitant and the whole passage might be printed as prose – as it was in the first Folio and still is in most modern editions. Yet in performance these lines work; they have that vitality and accuracy which are hall-marks of effective theatre.

The play has started with more than three hundred lines of talk, between two, three and, just before this wrestling match, four people. Duke Frederick and his court have come on stage specifically to witness the fight between Charles, the wrestler, and his unknown challenger – whom the audience knows as Orlando, who has already been seen in a mostly verbal fight with his brother Oliver. Shakespeare has contrived the dramatic exposition so that, in the silence as the contestants take the measure of each other, as much as possible will be at stake. Oliver has persuaded Charles that his brother is a dangerous villain and has encouraged him to fight to kill; Charles has just left three challengers for dead; Rosalind and Celia have openly favoured the unknown challenger, and have talked of love, sadness, fortune and folly; the Duke (who has usurped the throne of Rosalind's father, the true Duke) seems to pity Orlando and attempts to stop the fight; Orlando is in revolt against his brother who has brought him up as a peasant:

> obscuring and hiding from me all gentleman-like qualities. The spirit of my father grows strong in me, and I will no longer endure it   (I. i. 56–9)

– for him, it is a fight for freedom and opportunity. So much, at least, is packed into the odds of this moment of confrontation between Charles and Orlando in Duke Frederick's court. Now, as the stage fills and preparations for fighting and viewing go forward, the colour, movement, various rhythms and multiple sounds give the all-important and exciting sense of occasion and expectation which has hitherto been denied to the play: the action is now fully under way and the audience fully and precisely attentive.

But in the Folio text (which represents the earliest productions of the play) the brief stage-direction 'Wrestle' is followed four lines later by 'Shout', and then the dialogue printed above. The fight is over in a moment; everyone cries out; and it is clear that the young girls' wishes have been fulfilled as if by magic: the champion has been thrown, and lies as dead. This gives, for these six lines, a stunned silence: as the words are spoken, Le Beau and others attend to Charles and bear his great body away. Verbal economy is strict, Orlando's longer speech being left unanswered until line 191 when the Duke asks his name. He answers simply, but in doing so detonates another dramatic surprise: instead of commendation and reward, he is given nothing, and the stage empties even more quickly than it had just been filled. In seven lines, all but one of them running unbroken to the full length of the iambic pentameters, Duke Frederick has rejected the 'gallant' winner (199) because he is son of his 'enemy'. This hatred, or fear, that is released like a spring, is private, for as the Duke himself says: 'The world esteemed thy father honourable'.

Shakespeare could have given Frederick words with which to reveal or suggest the basis of his hatred, but his dramatic strategy here is to use the simplest words and nothing in the way of metaphor or decoration. Frederick's speech is amplified by repetitions, but the last line does not significantly add to the bare statement of the first, or of the fourth and fifth; the only development is that he has moved away from the bare expression of enmity towards a wish that it had not been disclosed. When the court has left the stage, and only Orlando, Rosalind, and Celia are left, the audience will expect clarification. They may also wonder where the play will lead, for as the Duke remains enigmatic, Oliver's plot against Orlando has fizzled out and Orlando has scarcely bettered himself; and the banished Duke has still not been viewed. The two girls dressed as princesses, and the 'young man' dressed as a 'hind' (I. i. 15) must stand at some distance from each other; they speak at first out of earshot:

DUKE FREDERICK: I would thou hadst been son to some man else.
  The world esteemed thy father honourable,
  But I did find him still mine enemy.   195
  Thou shouldst have better pleased me with this deed,
  Hadst thou descended from another house.
  But fare thee well, thou art a gallant youth;
  I would thou hadst told me of another father.
                    Exeunt Duke Frederick, [Le Beau and Lords]
CELIA: Were I my father, coz, would I do this?   200
ORLANDO: I am more proud to be Sir Rowland's son,
  His youngest son, and would not change that calling
  To be adopted heir to Frederick.
ROSALIND: My father loved Sir Rowland as his soul,
  And all the world was of my father's mind.   205
  Had I before known this young man his son,
  I should have given him tears unto entreaties,
  Ere he should thus have ventured.
CELIA: Gentle cousin,
  Let us go thank him, and encourage him.
  My father's rough and envious disposition   210
  Sticks me at heart. Sir, you have well deserved.
  If you do keep your promises in love
  But justly, as you have exceeded all promise,
  Your mistress shall be happy.

ROSALIND: Gentleman,
                 [*Gives him a chain from her neck*]
    Wear this for me, one out of suits with fortune,   215
    That could give more, but that her hand lacks means.
    Shall we go coz?
CELIA: Ay. Fare you well, fair gentleman.
ORLANDO: Can I not say, I thank you? My better parts
    Are all thrown down, and that which here stands up
    Is but a quintain, a mere lifeless block.   220
ROSALIND: He calls us back. My pride fell with my fortunes;
    I'll ask him what he would. Did you call sir?
    Sir, you have wrestled well, and overthrown
    More than your enemies.
CELIA: Will you go coz?
ROSALIND: Have with you. Fare you well.   225
                         Exeunt Rosalind [*and Celia*]
ORLANDO: What passion hangs these weights upon my tongue?
    I cannot speak to her, yet she urged conference.
    O poor Orlando, thou art overthrown.
    Or Charles, or something weaker, masters thee.

                    Enter LE BEAU

LE BEAU: Good sir, I do in friendship counsel you   230
    To leave this place. Albeit you have deserved
    High commendation, true applause, and love,
    Yet such is now the Duke's condition
    That he misconsters all that you have done.
    The Duke is humorous; what he is indeed,   235
    More suits you to conceive than I to speak of.
ORLANDO: I thank you sir; and pray you tell me this,
    Which of the two was daughter of the Duke
    That here was at the wrestling?
LE BEAU: Neither his daughter, if we judge by manners;   240
    But yet indeed the smaller is his daughter.
    The other is daughter to the banished Duke,
    And here detained by her usurping uncle,
    To keep his daughter company; whose loves
    Are dearer than the natural bond of sisters.   245
    But I can tell you that of late this Duke

Hath ta'en displeasure 'gainst his gentle niece,
Grounded upon no other argument
But that the people praise her for her virtues,
And pity her for her good father's sake; 250
And on my life his malice 'gainst the lady
Will suddenly break forth. Sir, fare you well.
Hereafter, in a better world than this,
I shall desire more love and knowledge of you.
ORLANDO: I rest much bounden to you; fare you well. 255
                                          [*Exit Le Beau*]
Thus must I from the smoke into the smother,
From tyrant Duke unto a tyrant brother:
But heavenly Rosalind!   *Exit*

As the audience concentrates attention on the three figures
remaining on stage after the general *exeunt*, the first response is
an unanswered question from Celia: 'Were I my father, coz,
would I do this?' She could hardly expect an answer, so her
words serve to show the girls' helplessness, and yet another clash
between kinspeople. Together these themes dominate the passage, with obtrusive repetition. The words 'father', 'son' and
'daughter' occur seventeen times, and there are numerous related
words such as *lord, name, liege, house, calling, heir, cousin, mistress,
coz, master, uncle, sister, niece, brother*; 'love' is used by all four
characters speaking in the scene after the Duke's *exit*. Celia's
question prompts and supports others, so that every character is
seen in kinship or subservience to others.

As speech becomes more generally sustained, images and
epithets are used sparingly, but to almost single purpose. Except
for 'out of suits with fortune' (215), all the word-play is on
various forms of attack and fight: 'sticks me at heart', 'thrown
down', 'stands up', 'quintain' (or mobile 'block' used in jousting),
'wrestled', 'overthrown' (twice). Orlando's 'What passion hangs
these weights upon my tongue?' (226) is related to these images by
referring to weights used as a handicap. Rosalind's

> Sir, you have wrestled well, and overthrown
> More than your enemies   (223-4)

uses the basic metaphor in the most complicated way, acknowledging a fight and defeat within herself and, by inference, utter-
ing her love through the complete disguise of 'enemies'. Besides
a continuing concern with family ties, the wrestling match has
awoken a recognition of personal struggle and of conflicts within
families. Without the near-naked, attention-catching fight and
its surprising outcome, these images would not have such immediate power. By restricting the allusiveness and extra-dramatic
reference of his language so rigorously to this one image, Shakespeare was cashing some of the dramatic capital won by his
physical *coup de théâtre*.

But grouping, movement, entries, exits, and the silences that
follow the silence of the fight, are the most potent elements in
Shakespeare's stagecraft in this scene. Leaving only three characters on stage, Shakespeare nevertheless prevents Orlando from
saying a word to either of the two girls. This is not so apparent
in a reading of the text as in a performance. Notice that Celia's
question to Rosalind is not answered; what follows is Orlando's
three lines proudly claiming allegiance to his father. These are not
spoken to either of the girls, but are his delayed answer to
Frederick, said for the sake of saying them. However, Rosalind
does overhear, and in her next speech echoes his words and
the earlier words of Frederick; she has been paying the closest
attention to Orlando, but clearly she does not yet speak to him,
for in line 206 he is still 'this young man' in the third person, and
Celia suggests that they '*go* thank him' (209). So far there is, in
fact, a double focus on the stage, on the girls and on Orlando,
neither party talking to the other, although Rosalind, at least, is
aware of the possibility. When Celia leads across the stage towards
Orlando, her words 'Sir, you have well deserved' seem to require
an answer; certainly her next, more informal lines, expressing a
greater freedom of mind, invite mutual confidence. But Orlando
is yet again silent, and it is now Rosalind who speaks and acts:
not waiting for him to respond to Celia, she gives a token that
he cannot do otherwise than acknowledge and take. Some communication has become absolutely necessary as he accepts the

gift, but it is unspoken: it must be a shared and silent recognition, which Rosalind's 'Shall we go coz?' (218) probably breaks off. Of course this phrase is spoken with an acted unconcern, but it (and Celia's simple 'Ay') does not suggest embarrassment; Celia leads away, across the stage, with a lightly-given compliment. The silent meeting was real and mutual; it displays awareness of each other's concern and a willingness to stand gazing upon each other. Shakespeare, by making it the silent outcome of exaggeratedly separate responses to other matters, has given it an impression of inevitability and strength, and also the interest of the unknown.

Only as Rosalind moves away can Orlando speak, still in soliloquy but now with rhythms cutting across the iambics. Rosalind also soliloquizes, perhaps after an aside to Celia; and, quickly, she again addresses Orlando: and she, too, has shorter, broken rhythms. At this point, Shakespeare repeats the device of silence: only this time it is Celia, in words echoing Rosalind's at the previous encounter, who breaks off the meeting; and it is Rosalind, now much more in possession of her wits, who speaks the simple 'Fare you well' at parting. Her concluding speech is an incomplete verse-line in a sequence of lines that all run to their full length, and so there is probably yet another silence before or after her last words. This is no longer a simple romantic silence, the first 'changing' of eyes, as Shakespeare has Prospero call it in *The Tempest* (I. ii. 441). They are 'Alike bewitched by the charm of looks' (*Romeo*, II Chorus), but now they are released, as well as captured, by what has happened. Rosalind finds a new and gentle confidence. Orlando, in the soliloquy he has on their departure, speaks with newly vigorous rhythms and wit, and with a self-conscious, ironic glee: the 'spirit of his father' has been 'strong in him', but he is now exultantly pleased to be 'mastered'.

When Le Beau enters with news of Frederick's dangerous enmity, Orlando thanks him politely but briefly, and then sets to work to find out who Rosalind may be. While he calls himself 'poor Orlando' (228), he is by no means the 'weaker' for meeting his match; and he has the wit to see this. Shakespeare has contrived the scene to show all this, not by verbal description but by the concerted effect of speech, movement, action and a series of silent confrontations that go with, and often surpass, the verbal drama.

Le Beau's re-entry is a complete surprise: nothing that this smooth courtier has said or done prepares for the risk he takes in bringing secret news of the Duke's intentions. Yet, after an abrupt and perhaps hurried beginning, his rhythms are smooth and well sustained; he neatly accomplishes his purpose and answers Orlando's enquiry. His last two lines suggest that the encounter is under pressure of other business in the Duke's presence. The whole is a reminder that humane concerns may operate underneath official or politically necessary behaviour. Here too is an unexpected meeting in trust, an echo, weaker in feeling but more explicit in words, of the meeting between Rosalind and Orlando. As the audience readjusts its perception of Le Beau, its adaptability in making other evaluations of character-involvement will be strengthened.

One is needed immediately, for Le Beau gives occasion for Orlando to show that he can be naturally and firmly courteous while his feelings run another way; he appreciates the service rendered to him, but his own danger is of less importance than the identity of Rosalind. At the same time he shows some resource, for he elicits the information he needs without mentioning his true interest. His concluding soliloquy shows a simple, though perhaps scornful, acceptance of his political and family misfortune, his joyous thoughts of 'heavenly Rosalind' counterbalancing everything else. His troubles are controlled in two smart antitheses; and then, surely, he must leap from the stage, his eyes and being alight with thoughts of love that are expressed in the simple: 'But heavenly Rosalind!' This joyful exit crowns the progressive presentation of Orlando. He is not a lover who talks at length to others or himself about his lady – verbally he has one apostrophe and some self-doubt – but in effect his love is strong, invigorating, and wholly re-orientating.

Shakespeare follows this scene with one more physical statement: as Orlando has left the stage alone, so Rosalind re-enters alone at the beginning of the following scene; but, unlike him, she is utterly silent. Celia however calls after her, and so Rosalind is aroused first to confess that she does not have one word 'to throw at a dog' – except those necessary to admit as much – and then to acknowledge her love through witty evasion. She does not praise Orlando but acknowledges her own madness (see line 7), helplessness and love with great energy of antithesis, pun, metaphor, paradox and comparison, and yet with an awareness that sees the approaching Duke before the less involved Celia can do so. Love's marks on Rosalind are imaginative and restless; complicated on the surface of words, yet intensely simple.

These lovers are bound to love fearlessly and deeply; now the play is alive with possibilities and the wrestling match with Charles has fully served its turn.

This is consummate exposition, and it is difficult to know what element of the dramatic style to praise most. Again, here are characters seemingly motivated from deep within their consciousness: the Duke, Le Beau, Orlando, Rosalind and the comparatively silent but quickly responsive Celia – each has an appropriate mode of presentation within this one short episode. There is variety and energy in stage activity, from a crowded court responding to a fatal wrestling match, to a tentative meeting of two individuals in silent and unexplored attraction, to a lone exultant exit and to a lone and silent entry. And all this variety, even the brief ejaculatory utterances, is held together by repeated words and images (and by consecutive iambic pentameters), so that love and politics, feeling and physical exertion, kinship and hidden enmity, are all received as emanations of a single view of men and women, power and helplessness. Perhaps the greatest achievement of the style is its variety and consummate ability to sound the right note in short compass, its combination of vivacity and sensitive human understanding.

Act IV, Scene I

ROSALIND: Why then, can one desire too much of a good thing? Come sister, you shall be the priest, and marry us. Give me your hand Orlando. What do you say sister?

ORLANDO: Pray thee marry us.

CELIA: I cannot say the words.   110

ROSALIND: You must begin, 'Will you Orlando –'

CELIA: Go to. Will you Orlando, have to wife this Rosalind?

ORLANDO: I will.

ROSALIND: Ay, but when?

ORLANDO: Why now, as fast as she can marry us.   115

ROSALIND: Then you must say, 'I take thee Rosalind for wife'.

ORLANDO: I take thee Rosalind, for wife.

ROSALIND: I might ask you for your commission, but I do take thee Orlando for my husband. There's a girl goes before the priest, and certainly a woman's thought runs before her actions.

ORLANDO: So do all thoughts, they are winged.   121

ROSALIND: Now tell me how long you would have her, after you have possessed her.

ORLANDO: For ever and a day.

ROSALIND: Say 'a day' without the 'ever'. No, no, Orlando, men are April when they woo, December when they wed. Maids are May when they are maids, but the sky changes when they are wives. I will be more jealous of thee than a Barbary cock-pigeon over his hen, more clamorous than a parrot against rain, more new-fangled than an ape, more giddy in my desires than a monkey. I will weep for nothing, like Diana in the fountain, and I will do that when you are disposed to be merry. I will laugh like a hyen, and that when thou art inclined to sleep.   133

ORLANDO: But will my Rosalind do so?

ROSALIND: By my life, she will do as I do.   135

ORLANDO: O but she is wise.

ROSALIND: Or else she could not have the wit to do this. The wiser, the waywarder. Make the doors upon a woman's wit, and it will out at the casement. Shut that and 'twill out at the key-hole. Stop that, 'twill fly with the smoke out at the chimney.   141

ORLANDO: A man that had a wife with such a wit, he might say 'Wit whither wilt?'

ROSALIND: Nay, you might keep that check for it till you met your wife's wit going to your neighbour's bed.   145

ORLANDO: And what wit could wit have to excuse that?

ROSALIND: Marry to say she came to seek you there. You shall never take her without her answer, unless you take her without her tongue. O that woman that cannot make her fault her husband's occasion, let her never nurse her child herself, for she will breed it like a fool.   151

ORLANDO: For these two hours Rosalind, I will leave thee.

ROSALIND: Alas, dear love, I cannot lack thee two hours.

ORLANDO: I must attend the duke at dinner, by two o'clock I will be with thee again.   155

ROSALIND: Ay, go your ways, go your ways; I knew what you would prove; my friends told me as much, and I thought no less. That flattering tongue of yours won me. 'Tis but one cast away, and so come, death. Two o'clock is your hour?

ORLANDO: Ay, sweet Rosalind.   160

ROSALIND: By my troth, and in good earnest, and so God mend me, and by all pretty oaths that are not dangerous, if you break one jot of your promise, or come one minute behind your hour, I will think you the most pathetical break-promise, and the most hollow lover, and the most unworthy of her you call Rosalind, that may be chosen out of the gross band of the unfaithful. Therefore beware my censure, and keep your promise.   167

ORLANDO: With no less religion than if thou wert indeed my Rosalind. So adieu.   169

ROSALIND: Well, time is the old justice that examines all such offenders, and let time try. Adieu.   *Exit Orlando*

CELIA: You have simply misused our sex in your love-prate. We must have your doublet and hose plucked over your head, and show the world what the bird hath done to her own nest.   174

ROSALIND: O coz, coz, coz, my pretty little coz, that thou didst know how many fathom deep I am in love. But it cannot be sounded; my affection hath an unknown bottom, like the bay of Portugal.

CELIA: Or rather bottomless, that as fast as you pour affection in, it runs out.   180

ROSALIND: No, that same wicked bastard of Venus, that was begot of thought, conceived of spleen and born of madness,

that blind rascally boy that abuses every one's eyes because his own are out, let him be judge how deep I am in love. I'll tell thee Aliena, I cannot be out of the sight of Orlando. I'll go find a shadow, and sigh till he come.   186
CELIA: And I'll sleep   *Exeunt*

In terms of action, or narrative, little is accomplished here: Rosalind, disguised as the shepherd Ganymede, pretends – rather inconsistently – to be Rosalind, proposes a pretended wedding, interrupts this and rails against matrimony; Orlando remembers an engagement with the Duke; and Rosalind and Celia are left for the former to confess her love once more and the latter to mock. Yet this episode is the climactic encounter between the heroine and hero of the comedy: how is this accomplished?

First, envisage the pretended 'wedding'; see and hear it. Rosalind finishes a run of word-play with a mocking compliment: speaking as Ganymede pretending to be Rosalind, she says Orlando is so 'good' a thing that she will have 'twenty such' (102). 'Why then' at the beginning of this concluding line, helps to give a crisp rhythm: two syllables, poised before a run of ten. The run itself has three main stresses: the first four syllables with a stress on 'desire', then 'too much' quite lightly, and a final four syllables, two very light but the last two bringing the sentence and the word-play begun several lines earlier to their end with 'good thing'. This last phrase is no new-minted verbal excitement, but a teasing and delighted ambiguity: 'a good thing' is a commodity, so that Orlando is treated as an object; it is an experience, so that Rosalind speaks of her delight in Orlando; and, with a look back to 'wilt thou have me?' of line 101, which is a phrase used often by Shakespeare of the act of love, it is sexual delight. The rhythm of Rosalind's first sentence: two, pause, four, two, four, with emphasis on the first, sixth and last two syllables, is assured and lightly alert; its main point is held for the concluding syllables that release the widest range of meaning and association. Orlando does not reply; and Rosalind does not continue. This does not only mean that she has silenced Orlando; she has also, momentarily, silenced herself, for at this point there is a change of subject that brings change of mood and of impersonation. Somewhere between the two sentences there is a moment of stillness and control, a rebalancing between completion and beginning; and this involves inward thoughts and feelings, and a decision about the next sequence of words and actions. The moment of stillness would be necessary if the talk were like a prescribed and formal dance; it is still more obligatory because it is, in dramatic fact, a brilliant improvisation.

After the moment of control, Ganymede continues as Ganymede, not Rosalind, keeping the 'lead' in the talk as much by the new brisk rhythm as by a new subject of attention. Commas and full-stops in the printed text suggest natural breaks, and there are probably slighter breaks before 'Orlando' and 'sister' (108) so that the sense is clear. On the page this is one continuous speech, but in reality it is three separate addresses. 'Come sister, you shall be the priest, and marry us' is to Celia, and draws her into the picture; it also breaks the closer (and, for Rosalind, perhaps more dangerous because more revealing) intimacy between Orlando and herself. Celia does not say anything in reply and Rosalind now speaks to Orlando: 'Give me your hand Orlando.' It is not clear what his response is; he may give his hand, she may take it, or there may be no outward response at all. Nor is it clear whether Ganymede, or Ganymede-Rosalind, or Rosalind herself is speaking. Certainly Rosalind must look again at Orlando, and he at her; and certainly Rosalind at once looks away again to Celia her cousin, whom she again calls 'sister', showing that Ganymede is speaking. Somewhere here there must have been a shared response between Orlando and Rosalind, but it lasts only a brief moment: were it longer, too much might be communicated. Now Orlando also looks away at Celia, accepting the proposed charade with 'Pray thee marry us.' Both lovers standing or, more probably, kneeling, wait for her response: Celia has the focus of attention on stage and in the auditorium, and she has been given the 'lead' in the talk. But at this point, comically, the pretence breaks down on Celia's admission 'I cannot say the words.' She may be laughing or be too much concerned; or she is just not ready for the impersonation. Possibly the two lovers who are kept waiting, kneeling side by side, will seem absurd, or helpless; certainly here is a moment when the play stands still, for a timed exposure. Celia's hesitation has revealed the quick eagerness of the other two, who in their imaginations can travel quickly all the way from the forest of Arden to a church, from self-commanding utterance to mutual silence.

Ganymede prompts Celia, but with her first few words only. Either Rosalind cannot bring herself to let Ganymede speak the more crucial 'have to wife this Rosalind', or else Celia's 'Go to' steps in to save her the task of proposing matrimony. Presumably Celia's priestly words are spoken with due – or exaggerated – formality, and Orlando answers in the same idiom, perhaps quite lightly, for he is looking at Celia and not at Ganymede-Rosalind, the one person who could disturb a simple response. The charade begins to run smoothly: but Rosalind, who proposed it, now disturbs it, speaking in quick rhythm and with revealing direct-ness: 'Ay, but when?' This question could hardly come from Ganymede or from Ganymede-Rosalind: this is Rosalind herself involuntarily expressing her doubt, impatience, helplessness, self-doubt. The exact expression – what involvement is betrayed – is a matter for experiment and choice during rehearsals; the three words are an open invitation for the actress (or in Shakespeare's day, boy-actor) to show a quick flush of true concern. It must be quick, for Orlando now speaks to Ganymede and Ganymede replies, speaking a similar formula to the one Rosalind had re-fused (or Celia spared her) five lines earlier: 'Then you must say, "I take thee Rosalind for wife".' It is possible that Rosalind broke into the 'ceremony' in order to propose this statement herself, unwilling to leave so much to Celia; certainly when Orlando turns to address Ganymede-Rosalind in the old and sanctified words, Rosalind does unambiguously usurp the priest's role:

I might ask you for your commission, but I do take thee Orlando
for my husband.   (118–19)

– and then confesses what she has done, perhaps through pride and excitement, perhaps as an excuse: 'There's a girl goes before the priest'. The rhythm of the excuse is light and easy although it grows in reference, from 'girl' to 'woman' and from 'goes' to 'runs', and therefore gives an increasingly strong expression of energy and understanding.

The nicety with which this episode is controlled by Shakespeare can be revealed only in careful and experimental rehearsal. Even if Orlando looks at Rosalind on 'Why now, as fast as he can marry us', it is still the more deliberate phrase of formal acceptance which must ensure the direct exchange of looks and understanding: 'I do take thee Rosalind, for wife.' A long silence can be sustained here, for after the word 'wife', Rosalind breaks the spell of the charade, not by a side-issue, but by running ahead. She does this partly through eagerness, and yet the first reference is to 'commission' (or licence, authority) that suggests doubt or defensiveness, or is, possibly, a delighted, playful excuse.

The actress will choose which of the available *personae* speaks in the crucial speech. Ganymede-Rosalind may say 'I do take thee Orlando for my husband', and Ganymede the rest. Yet somewhere Rosalind is liable to speak for herself, since her voice has almost certainly been heard earlier with 'good thing' or 'Ay, but when?', or at least her reaction has been made obvious in a held silence. Rosalind herself may speak the acceptance of 'my husband', half-involuntarily; or, Rosalind's true voice may not be heard until the comment and excuse, consciously deciding to speak her mind because she has realized that Orlando is caught up in the imaginative fiction.

Whoever speaks her last words – 'certainly a woman's thought runs before her actions' – Orlando must hear them, for he takes up her meaning, identifying himself with that response and extending the image from running to levitation, and from immediate to far-ranging reference: 'So do all thoughts, they are winged.' All his imagination is alive, so that where no response is needed he joins in, leaving the key word to last so that his more general idea does not lack precision. As on 'good thing' (107), Rosalind again breaks off the talk to begin again; but this time it

D

is Orlando's thought that has disturbed her rather than her own, and she reveals, not growing confidence, but some kind of doubt:

> Now tell me how long you would have her after you have pos-
> sessed her. (122–3)

A new movement of the duologue, Celia again forgotten, must now begin; and it is wide open for Orlando to say whatever is in his mind: Rosalind is taking a bigger risk.

To discover the theatrical life of this dialogue, its excitement, weight and point, it is necessary to ask why each word is spoken, to whom, and how: these questions reveal the changing consciousness of the individual characters and the innermost interplay between them; they begin to distinguish between considered and involuntary utterances, and to chart the changing focus of attention. Clearly this is a scene of major importance in the drama, but not because anything is achieved towards the completion of a plot, and not because of brilliant verbal statement; in performance it is the exposure and meeting of two invented characters giving a climactic impression of inward and outward, conscious and unconscious, individual and shared response. It needs expressive, open, alert, and sensitive acting.

Hitherto there have been few metaphors, similes or verbal complexities; now, from Rosalind, the language leaps, turns, strides and hesitates, so that it expresses physical, sensual and intellectual energy. She has dared to look ahead beyond marriage, while Orlando has answered conventionally, in fairy-tale terms. She probably answers as Ganymede, who had professed the ability to 'cure' Orlando of his love; but in mocking the man, she finds that she herself is involved as the 'maid' (126). The result is a sustained account of Rosalind as a wife which leaves Orlando bewildered. On one level it offers a depressing prospect: thunder, jealousy, masculine stridency, intemperate and stupid noise, vicissitudes and near madness: this Rosalind will be unfeeling, importunate and perverse. But by naming such faults, Rosalind releases her inner excitement so that, by varied and sustained rhythms alone, the speech is compulsively attractive; to speak in this manner requires confidence, and delight.

Consider, first, the units or phrases of speech. The preliminary response (125) takes Orlando's words and contradicts them without fuss in a slightly longer phrase, pointed by the 'without' in the middle. Then quickly come the two monosyllables of denial and Orlando's name; this is a light yet countering rhythm which is followed by a double, balanced phrase, partly echoing the double phrasing of 'For ever and a day', but extending it and marking a more reflective balance by the closeness in sound between 'when they woo' and 'when they wed' at the end of each element. Echoing sense as well as phrasing, the next sentence grows in power, partly by the alliteration and repetition within '*Maids* are *May* when they are *maids*', and still more by the change to 'but the sky changes' which both extends the image and changes the rhythm; this new element is contained within the same general rhythmic pattern by the concluding 'when they are wives'. The image of the sky is ambiguous in effect; certainly the sky seems to threaten, but it also releases the statement from a particular to more general reference. From this moment a new rhythm is introduced, led off by a pronoun, in the first person singular: '*I* will be . . .' This new sentence moves in four units, each growing shorter and firmer up to the third, and then extending in length and lightening for the fourth. Vowel sounds broaden, sharpen and then, in the fourth phrase, lighten. At the conclusion of the speech, rhythms are more sustained; first a sentence of three phrases, the first and last with similar introductions, and then a compact variation of the same pattern. The last sentence contains references to both hyena-like laughter and a husband's inclination to sleep; yet it ends quietly and neatly. At this point Rosalind has no more to say and she relinquishes the lead to Orlando. Yet she regains it at once with the dramatic irony of the assertive, yet simply phrased, 'By my life, she will do as I do.' To give effect to Ganymede's voice and to Rosalind's voice in this short sentence will need nice judgement and a fairly slow tempo: this line must stand over against the whole catalogue that has preceded it.

When we consider how the speech will sound we may become aware of its restless and yet confident energy, and its sense of completion. If we then ask *why* it is spoken, its effect may be more fully realized. After the quick antitheses whereby Rosalind establishes Ganymede's scepticism concerning Orlando's protestation, she thinks of herself, and the line of imagery breaks for the threatening yet extended reference to the 'sky' (127); and, once given this freedom, her imagination rushes on. Somewhere she decides to speak as Ganymede-Rosalind or, even, for herself; perhaps on the second 'maids' (127), and certainly before 'I' (128). So the wider reference leads, paradoxically, to the individual, but to an imagined, fanciful individual: the wife Rosalind has not yet become. Jealousy comes first to mind, presumably suggested by fear and a sense of inadequacy; yet this is no cold passion, for the 'Barbary cock-pigeon' is a strange, primitive, proud and pugnacious creature, and at the same time domestic, especially when the word 'hen' is introduced. 'Clamorous' as 'a parrot against rain', continues the bird-like and exotic references, and becomes comic by suggesting disproportion and utter ineffectiveness. 'More new-fangled than an ape', turns from birds to beasts, continuing the note of mockery and turning towards human beings in general through the very fashionable word 'new-fangled' and the likeness of ape to man. Here too is a restlessness, so that clearly Rosalind, in fancying herself a wife, finds her responses changing incessantly: it is this element which leads on to the end of the series of similitudes with 'giddy' (130). And now sexual 'desires' are uppermost in her mind, for this is what 'monkey' clearly introduces; it is a familiar comparison, as in *Henry IV, Part II*, 'as lecherous as a monkey' (III. ii. 238) or *Othello*, 'as hot as monkeys' (III. iii. 403). The epithet 'giddy' sustains the comic note and seems to belittle the 'desires' even as they are acknowledged; it is the fourth comparative in a row and the first to have a diminutive effect.

Why do the catalogue and the comparatives stop here, with the 'monkey'? Rosalind now imagines herself 'weeping', and her next image introduces the chaste Diana, and as a stone statue too. The

run of subtextual consciousness from cock and hen, through the
parading colour and noise of the parrot to ape and monkey, has
stopped; or it has been deflected from its course. Is Rosalind in
fact weeping 'for nothing', for joy, fear and hope? She certainly
comes close enough to tears to think of them in her awakened,
sportful imagination. We may now notice that each of the four
elements in the just completed catalogue might have involved
impossibility or unfulfilment: birds are not faithful mates, parrots
will never stop the rain, fashion always dies and in giddiness
nothing is assured; now the statue of Diana weeps for ever.
Possibly 'I will do that when you are disposed to be merry' is an
afterthought; Ganymede coming to the rescue of the true Rosalind, turning tears to laughter. Again I think that Ganymede-
Rosalind could, actually, turn quickly and excitedly to laughter,
as a defence or as another involuntary expression of her inward,
wholly new, sexual consciousness and fancy. A hyena is the most
completely bestial and the most stupid creature in Rosalind's
bestiary; and it is teamed defiantly with an image of Orlando
'inclined to sleep', that is, with Orlando in bed. So the last
sentence does stretch back in references to the 'desires' of line 130
and the 'maids' of 127; and perhaps to 'possessed' of line 123.
Rosalind has no more to say, now; she is sexually and affection-
ately awake, and in her imagination is in the still unrealized,
strange, tender and overwhelming world of Orlando's love for
her. We have seen already that rhythmically her next speech,
after Orlando's bemused question, must be large enough to stand
over against her previous tirade, and to speak for Rosalind as well
as Ganymede. Now we must add that it cannot be calculating or
arch: it expresses the simple, joyous confidence that is the other
side of the helpless, laughing hyena. By bringing these two
speeches so close together, Shakespeare reveals Rosalind's love in
sensitive and exciting climax.

To answer Ganymede, Orlando states the opposite: 'O but she
is wise' (136), and gladly Ganymede-Rosalind accepts the contra-
diction. In her apparent folly she wants to believe that she is wise;
she has no other wisdom. With quickening rhythms and brisk

paradox, she now plays for 'wit', for repartee. The sexual bird and
beast images almost wholly disappear. When, in lines 144-5, she
speaks of 'your wife's wit going to your neighbour's bed', it is
a commonplace innuendo without any indication of sensual
sub-textual involvement. In short, Rosalind now plays lightly and
even crudely. The only precise visual image is of 'smoke' rising
'out at the chimney', escaping into the air: and she in a sense is
doing just this, and also covering up her tracks in a vulgar smoke-
screen. Orlando appropriately answers with a proverb – 'your
tongue will run away with you' – and with paradoxical but very
simple word-play on 'wit' (146). Both his contributions are posed
as questions, and are thus in direct contrast to his next speech,
which is the statement: 'For these two hours Rosalind, I will leave
thee.' His mind has not been fully engaged in Rosalind's retreat
from too great an expression of feeling: if she does not hold him
with her fantasy, he has duties elsewhere that come to mind.

The scene looks as if it will run down, but Orlando's detachment sparks off an immediate reply: 'Alas, dear love, I cannot lack
thee two hours.' This is the first time Rosalind has called Orlando
anything but simply his name or 'you': her suddenly direct
expression of affection in 'dear love' is very simple, and all the
more revealing for that – without artifice or disguise, and almost
certainly without her volition. The bare repetition of his 'two
hours', may suggest that hers is a stunned response; but 'I cannot
lack thee' shows some self-awareness, even as it acknowledges
loss and incredulity. By the time Orlando has explained that he
is going to serve Rosalind's father, she is able to reassume the role
of Ganymede-Rosalind. The effect of the sudden exposure is now
expressed in more assertive, shorter rhythms, and in repetitions.
Quickly she tries a mocking acceptance of 'death'; but then is
caught back to her actual predicament so that she asks precisely:
'Two o'clock is your hour?'

Shakespeare contrives a long exit for Orlando which brings him
clearly into focus. First, he has a simple agreement, but with the
endearment 'sweet' attached to Rosalind's name (160). Then

Rosalind, in by far her longest sentence in this passage and a catalogue of three superlatives, threatens him with her ill opinion: this is the only weapon she has with which to defend herself, but she brings the speech to an end with a firmer, two-phrased rhythm and a mock heroic tone: 'Therefore beware my censure, and keep your promise.' The whole must be directed at Orlando, and he has no opportunity of reply until she is done. For some time both must have been standing; certainly by line 160 Orlando has already begun to move away. So the audience plainly sees that she is holding him back; that she is dependent on him and therefore piling conjuration and abjuration on him with equal energy. His reply when it comes has contrasting rhythm, and picks up her semi-religious reference to the 'band of the unfaithful' (166-7). She had added 'gross', which is a challenging quibble on 'numerous', 'ignorant', 'unfeeling' and, possibly, 'obscene', but he uses 'religion' quite simply, as if with complete faithfulness to the basic image. The ambiguity in his speech comes later, in 'if thou wert indeed my Rosalind'. Some actors here suggest that they have seen through the disguise, recognizing Rosalind. But this leads to difficulties, not least that of Orlando leaving the stage without suggesting a cruel desire to tease. Rather Orlando should still be deceived in his conscious mind and seem to half sense that he *has been* shown the true Rosalind. By allowing him to allude so ambiguously, at this point, to the trick that has been played on him, Shakespeare has ensured that, at the end of their encounter, the audience becomes aware of Orlando's thoughts and feelings as well as Rosalind's. He has also drawn attention to the fugitive nature of the reality that has existed under the words and apparently under the skin of the two characters: the pressure of conflicting meanings in a single word, the undeviating course of feeling under the quick and varying words, the excitement, fear, and confidence in the very sound of what has been said. Finally, in Rosalind's last words to Orlando, while he is silent, on the brink of breaking off contact with 'sweet Rosalind', Shakespeare has invited the audience to think ahead and sense that Rosalind quite as much as Orlando must leave profit and loss to 'time . . .

the old justice', as must all 'offenders'. Orlando is silent on his actual exit, so that Rosalind's involvement may well seem more at the mercy of what time brings than his; it is she that persists in 'examination'.

When he has gone, she is silent so that in her own time Celia can speak her following line that strips all disguise and takes earlier words at their bare value. In picking up the image of birds, Celia shows Rosalind to be helpless; in specifically referring to the disguising clothes she imagines them 'plucked' over the head – that is the wisdom – of Rosalind. After the abjurations of Rosalind's last speeches, Celia's rhythms sound sustained though light, perfectly in control. Her speech finishes on 'nest', neatly touching the secret centre of Rosalind's desires. There will be laughter in the audience, and probably on the stage as well, for tensions, reserves, hopes and fears are resolved into quick and affectionate intimacy. Rosalind's first sentence has tripping rhythm, delight in her 'pretty little coz' and a slower, simple end, 'deep . . . in love': and then she is able, again, to mock, to laugh at herself and acknowledge that she cannot say ('sounded', line 177) what has happened to her. Celia joins in the outlandish, lumpish word-play, and then Rosalind passes on to deprecate love in temperamental and half-crazy terms until she returns once more to the simple 'how deep I am in love'. Metaphorically and literally there is no holding her: she recovers, for the moment, her Ganymede impersonation to call Celia 'Aliena' (185) and then goes off stage to hide herself from herself, in a 'shadow'. She will have no more words but 'sigh till he come' (186). With a short, crisp phrase, Celia is given the last word, as she goes off, presumably in the opposite direction: 'And I'll sleep.' At the end of the scene, the drama is finely weighed and left in abeyance.

As the two girls leave with their own, now private, thoughts, 'Enter Jaques and Lords, Foresters', as the Folio stage-direction reads. A deer has been killed, and victory is proclaimed in a rousing song – ''tis no matter how it be in tune, so it make noise enough' (IV. ii. 7–8) – that takes bawdy pleasure in crowning the killer in the deer's still-bloody skin and the deer's horns. The fanciful and incomplete nature of Rosalind's encounter with her 'dear love' is thus made evident by strong contrast. The violence of this juxtaposition has been prepared for sufficiently to make it seem apt (without sacrificing the surprise) by Rosalind's picture of herself as 'but one cast away, and so come, death' (158–59), by the beast imagery and by the common talk of a cuckolded husband.

Though the strands of the narrative are many and for much of the time quite separate, *As You Like It* is a comedy in which each scene is tied to its fellows by words and actions. The overall dramatic impression is unusually complex, but by the last scene the very varied figures in the tableau are mutually defining. This is an element of the dramatic style that does not show readily in considering a single episode. Here let it be indicated by placing some of Rosalind's words, feelings and situation in this scene over against those of Touchstone, William and Audrey:

ORLANDO: O but she is wise.
ROSALIND: Or else she could not have the wit to do this. The wiser, the waywarder . . . You shall never take her without her answer, unless you take her without her tongue.

TOUCHSTONE: . . . Art thou wise?
WILLIAM: Ay sir, I have a pretty wit.
TOUCHSTONE: Why, thou sayest well. I do now remember a saying, 'The fool doth think he is wise, but the wise man knows himself to be a fool' . . .   (V. i. 26 ff.)

Rosalind accepts wisdom, but as a kind of foolishness. Rosalind admits she is witty and so does William, but he does not explain how this can be true. Touchstone doubts wisdom; Orlando trusts it. The duologue between Orlando and Rosalind raises laughable fooling about hope and satisfaction as well as about wisdom and folly; and it is not surprising that Touchstone continues, without hesitation:

The heathen philosopher, when he had a desire to eat a grape, would open his lips when he put it into his mouth; meaning thereby that grapes were made to eat, and lips to open. You do love this maid?

WILLIAM: I do sir.
TOUCHSTONE: Give me your hand. Art thou learned?
WILLIAM: No sir.

By echoes between scenes, Shakespeare not only relates episode to
episode but also encourages the audience to question the simple
needs within the glancing dialogue, to be awake to the complex
disguises. Such verbal correspondences cannot be relied upon to
make their points at every opportunity; nor is it necessary that
they should. But as the audience catches one here and another
there, an inviting and fanciful perspective begins to be established
in their minds.

Act V, Scene iv

Enter, HYMEN, ROSALIND *and* CELIA. *Still Music*

HYMEN: Then is there mirth in heaven,
  When earthly things made even
    Atone together.
  Good duke receive thy daughter,   100
  Hymen from heaven brought her,
    Yea brought her hither,
  That thou mightst join her hand with his
  Whose heart within her bosom is.
ROSALIND: [*To Duke*] To you I give myself, for I am yours.
  [*To Orlando*] To you I give myself, for I am yours.   106
DUKE SENIOR: If there be truth in sight, you are my daughter.
ORLANDO: If there be truth in sight, you are my Rosalind.
PHEBE: If sight and shape be true,
  Why then my love adieu.   110
ROSALIND: I'll have no father, if you be not he.
  I'll have no husband, if you be not he.
  Nor ne'er wed woman, if you be not she.
HYMEN: Peace ho, I bar confusion,
    'Tis I must make conclusion   115
      Of these most strange events.
  Here's eight that must take hands
  To join in Hymen's bands,
    If truth holds true contents.

You and you no cross shall part.   120
You and you are heart in heart.
You to his love must accord,
Or have a woman to your lord.
You and you are sure together,
As the winter to foul weather.   125
Whiles a wedlock hymn we sing,
Feed yourselves with questioning,
That reason wonder may diminish,
How thus we met, and these things finish.

HYMEN *and train* [*sing*]

Wedding is great Juno's crown,   130
     O blessed bond of board and bed.
'Tis Hymen peoples every town,
     High wedlock then be honoured.
Honour, high honour, and renown,
To Hymen, god of every town!   135

DUKE SENIOR: O my dear niece, welcome thou art to me.
     Even daughter, welcome in no less degree.
PHEBE: I will not eat my word, now thou art mine;
     Thy faith my fancy to thee doth combine.

For the end of the play, with Rosalind and Celia ready to drop their disguises, four couples ready to be married, and the Banished Duke ripe for restitution to his power, Shakespeare introduced some entirely new elements. There has been a series of songs throughout the scenes set in Arden, but now there comes '*Still Music*', formal and calm, and with no textual preparation at all. When it is first heard the audience will be taken by surprise and wonder who plays it, and where. Then the second surprise: the entry of a god, Hymen, with a train of attendants walking slowly with the music (or possibly dancing), and taking up a central position. The god then addresses the assembled company and also the Duke, who has until this moment been the commanding figure. A great variety of costume has been seen during the play – courtiers, shepherds, goatherds, clowns (natural and cultivated), wrestlers, servants, foresters, attendants, a priest – but the god making a masque-like entry, splendid and formal, is an innovation; visually he does not belong here. Since Shakespeare associated Hymen with tapers or torches in two other plays,[1] his train may well carry them here – another innovation.

There has been variety of speech in the play – prose, blank verse, couplets – but the short emphatically stressed and rhymed lines that Hymen speaks and sings have been used before only by Orlando in his bad verses and by Touchstone in his extempore mocking of them. Hymen's speeches, following the lively prose exchanges, are clear and solemn, and backed by the still music: they effect a huge change of rhythm and weight in a moment, producing a modulation without precedent. (Analogous devices are the play-within-the-play in *Hamlet*, or the theophanies of Shakespeare's last plays in which gods give judgement or blessing.)

Slow and measured speaking, decisive and unambiguous, without trace of subtextual qualification or counterstatement, will give emphasis to many words of wide significance. In the first three lines, *mirth, heaven, earthly, even, atone*, stand strongly within the metrical and rhyme schemes. Of these 'mirth' and 'heaven' have been heard before, but 'earthly' and 'atone' (or 'reconcile'; the literal meaning of 'make at one' was uppermost in Shakespeare's usage of this word) introduce new concepts. 'Even' (or 'equable', 'agreeable'), which gives the first rhyme, has been introduced earlier by Rosalind at the beginning of this last scene: 'I have promised to make all this matter even', and 'To make these doubts all even' (18 and 25), and these promises are now echoed in their fulfilment.[2] The beginning of Hymen's second speech, when he silences the human responses, picks up the ideas of 'made even'

---

[1] Cf. *Titus Andronicus*, I. i. 325, and *The Tempest*, IV. i. 23 and 97.

[2] This gives some support to the notion that Rosalind has written Hymen's words and prepared an actor to speak them – Corin is the obvious candidate, for he does not join the final scene in his own person. If so, there is perhaps an irony in recollecting the one scene in which he has dominated attention, where Touchstone reprimands him for bringing 'the ewes and the rams together' (III. ii. 69 ff.). If this notion is correct, Corin is unique among the amateur actors in Shakespeare's plays in that he completes his impersonation without slip or interruption; the godlike image is unquestioned.

and 'atone' in the more general word 'peace', and then introduces on the rhyme two further words that are new to the play: *con-fusion* and *conclusion*. The phrase 'these most strange events' is not entirely new, but looks back to the conclusion of Jaques's account of the Seven Ages of Man:

> Last scene of all
> That ends this strange eventful history,
> Is second childishness . . .   (II. vii. 162–5)

Hymen's speeches are generally without word-play, but there are two significant exceptions. First, speaking to Touchstone and Audrey, he likens their union to that between 'winter' and 'foul weather' and so echoes the first two songs by Amiens:

> Under the greenwood tree . . .
> Come hither, come hither, come hither.
> Here shall he see
> No enemy
> But winter and rough weather.   (II. v. 1–8 etc.)

and

> Blow, blow, thou winter wind,
> Thou are not so unkind
>   As man's ingratitude; . . . (II. vii. 173–89)

He also offers a contrasting image to that of the two young pages who had sung for Touchstone and Audrey immediately before this last scene:

> It was a lover and his lass, . . .
> That o'er the green corn-field did pass,
>   In the spring time, the only pretty ring time,
> When birds do sing, hey ding a ding, ding,
> Sweet lovers love the spring.   (V. iii. 14–31)

This song had been 'clapped into' roundly, 'like two gypsies on a horse' (9–13).

Elsewhere, Hymen's address to individuals touches with assurance upon the great commonplaces of love-stories, with rhymes on *his, hands, bands, heart, lord, together*. At the end of his second general speech, however, he uses his single punning line which touches on the subjective and hidden elements of love, and gives a reverberating echo of the inward excitement and danger that has filled the great love-making scenes of this comedy. At one level, the clinching line of the stanza is trite:

If truth holds true contents.   (119)

What should 'truth' (or troth) contain but truth? But 'contents' (that which is contained) also means contentments: as they pledge their truths (as the marriage vows have it) 'to have and to *hold*', will they be truly content? The last word alludes, in effect, to the title of the play: 'As You Like It'. It also gives direct verbal echoes of significant moments in the play. The first use of 'content' was when Celia and Rosalind decided to go to the forest of Arden, and it there alluded to pastoral happiness, closing the third scene on a couplet:

Now go we in content
To liberty and not to banishment.   (I. iii. 130-1)

The second use was more practical, being Orlando's last word, again on a couplet, as he goes to Arden:

And ere we have thy youthful wages spent
We'll light upon some settled low content.
(II. iii. 67-8)

Touchstone, Corin and Audrey all used the word in Arden itself:

> When I was at home, I was in a better place: but travellers must be *content*.   (II. iv. 13-15)

> He that wants money, means, and *content* is without three good friends ... Glad of other men's good, *content* with my harm ...
> (III. ii. 22-3 and 65-6)

> Doth my simple feature *content* you?   (III. iii. 2-3)

Finally Rosalind herself, as she promises to bring the stories to happy endings, uses it twice:

> I will *content* you, if what pleases you *contents* you, and you shall be married tomorrow.   (V. ii. 105-6)

For Shakespeare the word could express the deepest psychological issues. He had used it a year or so earlier in *The Merchant of Venice*, for Shylock's heavily ironic 'I am *content*' as he leaves the law-court defeated. The crux of the King's wooing of Katharine in *Henry V* comes with:

> – It shall please him, Kate.
> – Then it shall also *content* me.   (V. ii. 230-2)

In *Othello* it is used repeatedly and crucially, as in the Moor's

> I cannot speak enough of this *content*;
> It stops me here . . .   (II. i. 194-5)

An entry like Hymen's, so impressively prepared for and presented, so full of motto-like statements, invites the closest attention to words. Without an oracular, unclouded delivery, Hymen's words would merely tinkle with repetition, simple metre and rhyme; he would be a pompous, useless intrusion to the comedy, a mere dramatic convenience. But when his lines are spoken with proper weight and solemnity, individual words may drop like stones into the still water of the posed and held dramatic situation; the regularity of the grouping in pairs, the cessation of narrative uncertainty, the assurance and calm of the 'still music', alike give the smooth surface in which the last ripple of each significant word may be part of the achieved effect.

The various interjections of Rosalind, the Duke, Orlando and Phebe, which are given sharp definition and rhythm by repeated antitheses, ensure that the individual dramatic issues are not totally submerged in too easy and comprehensive a reconciliation by a machine-like god. With each spoken contribution, a different pair of the assembled company is drawn into focus. During the first exchanges the speakers see but do not touch each other – hence the repetition of 'sight', the continuous doubts expressed by the three 'if's' that begin three consecutive speeches, and the conscious reticence of Rosalind's three 'if's' in her second speech. At this point, 'confusion' is still possible, but when Hymen has addressed each pair individually and invited them to 'take hands' – it is here that they touch each other – the 'conclusion' is effected.

They are now silent, held by the 'truth' that each finds in the meetings: again the drama has been brought to an issue that lies beneath, and beyond, words, and yet is precisely individualized.

The echo that the repeated 'if's' bring of Touchstone's immediately preceding speech about quarrels shows the way ahead. His quarrellers had been imagined reaching the 'Lie Direct', and then avoiding even that 'with an If':

> as, 'If you said so, then I said so'; and they shook hands and swore brothers. Your If is the only peace-maker; much virtue in If.
>
> (86–92)

There are 'if's' in plenty when Hymen appears, and no disposition to quarrel; nevertheless, he has to call for 'Peace' (114) and before drawing the lovers together poses his own 'if':

> Here's eight that must take hands
> To join in Hymen's bands,
>   *If* truth holds true contents.

In silence his condition may be satisfied. There are no more 'if's'; only a recognition by the god that they should 'feed' themselves 'with questioning' – the physical metaphor stands strongly in the context:

> That reason wonder may diminish,
> How thus we met, and these things finish.

In this silence a song is sung by Hymen and his train, so that the individual situations, full of wonder and, at least for Touchstone and Audrey, full of laughter as well, are once more related to general and ordinary 'events'.

The last song follows others about idleness, pleasure, ingratitude and forgetfulness that have been sung by Amiens; it follows Jaques's parodying song of folly, Touchstone's country song of refusal, the Foresters' bawdy song of the 'lusty horn' and laughter, and the two pages' song of the spring time. For this song, tone and measure are wholly different, and the singing is probably in unison. Its words refer to mythical Juno, high honour and renown; but it is also a song for everybody, for 'Hymen peoples

every town' (132). After courtship and liberty, here is a song
of 'wedlock' looking forward to fertility and to the rights of
matrimony. 'O blessed bond of board and bed' refers specifically
to ancient rites, as recorded in the *York Manual* as early as 1403:

> Here I take thee . . . (name), to be my wedded wyfe, to hald and
> to haue at bed and at borde, for fayrer for layther, for better for
> wers . . . till ded us depart.

The comedy here touches upon the lives or prospects of each
individual member of the audience.

The lines of the Duke and Phebe that follow the song express
individual resolutions still further, and show that the focus has
become particular again immediately before the second son of old
Sir Rowland, Orlando's brother and Oliver's, comes with news
of the repentance of Frederick, the usurping Duke. Jaques then
comes to the forefront to give his more objective judgements,
and leaves before the celebration of matrimony and good fortune
in 'rustic revelry' (166). This exit is an important element of the
close, for it sharpens the focus once more upon individuals and
reminds the audience of the confusion and peace that wait at either
side of Hymen's and Touchstone's 'if's':

> Proceed, proceed. We will *begin* these rites,
> As we do *trust* they'll *end*, in *true* delights.   (186–7)

Because of the arrested moment, contrived through Hymen's impressive and unifying entry, the audience will hear these words in
a large context: the rites will be fortunate 'If truth holds true
contents', if all is, truly, as the characters individually and cor-
porately 'like it'.

3 Julius Caesar

IN THE theatre *Julius Caesar* has a twin reputation, first for three or four roles – Brutus, Cassius, Antony and Caesar – that give scope for impressive acting and various interpretations, and secondly for large ensemble scenes with the crowd in Rome, the assembling conspirators and then the battle formations. It is a good 'company play', full of detailed dramatic life and plenty of opportunities, large and small, for the actors. In the twentieth century it has also given scope for individualistic productions, realized with scenic originality or interpreted with seemingly new political or psychological slants.

The passages chosen for analysis are long enough to include both intensely personal drama and large-scale stage effects, so that Shakespeare's handling of the twin modes of this play may be observed. The bare, severe style of these passages is representative of the play as a whole, and seems to serve an overall ironic, intellectual or, even, ambiguous dramatic purpose; this is not so much a 'problem' or argumentative play, but one in which the audience's sympathy and understanding are constantly alerted and nicely poised.

Act I, Scene ii

Enter CAESAR, ANTONY *for the course,* CALPHURNIA, PORTIA, DECIUS, CICERO, BRUTUS, CASSIUS, CASCA, *a* SOOTHSAYER; *after them* MARULLUS *and* FLAVIUS [*and others*]

CAESAR: Calphurnia.
CASCA: Peace ho! Caesar speaks.
CAESAR: Calphurnia.
CALPHURNIA: Here my lord.

CAESAR: Stand you directly in Antonius' way,
　　When he doth run his course. Antonius.
ANTONY: Caesar, my lord?   5
CAESAR: Forget not, in your speed, Antonius,
　　To touch Calphurnia; for our elders say,
　　The barren, touched in this holy chase,
　　Shake off their sterile curse.
ANTONY:　　　　　　　　I shall remember.
　　When Caesar says, 'Do this', it is performed.   10
CAESAR: Set on, and leave no ceremony out.
SOOTHSAYER: Caesar!
CAESAR: Ha! Who calls?
CASCA: Bid every noise be still. Peace yet again!
CAESAR: Who is it in the press that calls on me?   15
　　I hear a tongue shriller than all the music
　　Cry 'Caesar!' Speak; Caesar is turned to hear.
SOOTHSAYER: Beware the ides of March.
CAESAR:　　　　　　　　　　　What man is that?
BRUTUS: A soothsayer bids you beware the ides of March.
CAESAR: Set him before me, let me see his face.   20
CASSIUS: Fellow, come from the throng, look upon Caesar.
CAESAR: What say'st thou to me now? Speak once again.
SOOTHSAYER: Beware the ides of March.
CAESAR: He is a dreamer, let us leave him. Pass.
　　　　　　　　　　Sennet. Exeunt all except Brutus and Cassius
CASSIUS: Will you go see the order of the course?   25
BRUTUS: Not I.
CASSIUS: I pray you do.
BRUTUS: I am not gamesome; I do lack some part
　　Of that quick spirit that is in Antony.
　　Let me not hinder, Cassius, your desires;   30
　　I'll leave you.
CASSIUS: Brutus, I do observe you now of late;
　　I have not from your eyes that gentleness
　　And show of love as I was wont to have.
　　You bear too stubborn and too strange a hand   35
　　Over your friend that loves you.
BRUTUS:　　　　　　　　　　Cassius,
　　Be not deceived. If I have veiled my look,

I turn the trouble of my countenance
Merely upon myself. Vexed I am
Of late with passions of some difference,   40
Conceptions only proper to myself,
Which give some soil perhaps to my behaviours.
But let not therefore my good friends be grieved –
Among which number, Cassius, be you one –
Nor construe any further my neglect,   45
Than that poor Brutus with himself at war,
Forgets the shows of love to other men.
CASSIUS: Then Brutus, I have much mistook your passion;
By means whereof this breast of mine hath buried
Thoughts of great value, worthy cogitations.   50
Tell me good Brutus, can you see your face?
BRUTUS: No Cassius; for the eye sees not itself
But by reflection, by some other things.
CASSIUS: 'Tis just;
And it is very much lamented Brutus,   55
That you have no such mirrors as will turn
Your hidden worthiness into your eye,
That you might see your shadow. I have heard,
Where many of the best respect in Rome –
Except immortal Caesar – speaking of Brutus,   60
And groaning underneath this age's yoke,
Have wished that noble Brutus had his eyes.
BRUTUS: Into what dangers would you lead me Cassius,
That you would have me seek into myself
For that which is not in me?   65

Julius Caesar was accounted the foremost man of ancient times,
scholar, soldier and Emperor. In the first scene of the play named
after him, Shakespeare has two tribunes, or representatives of the
people, leave the stage fearing that Caesar will

> soar above the view of men,
> And keep us all in servile fearfulness.

Caesar now enters for the first time, with some musical accompaniment (see line 16 and the 'Sennet', or trumpet-call, with which
the Folio text directs him to leave) and a 'press' or 'throng' (15

and 21) of people around him. He is celebrating the Feast of
Lupercal (a festival of purification and fertility) and his own victory in Spain over the sons and followers of Pompey (whom he
had earlier defeated in civil war). With him are his wife, Mark
Antony, Brutus, Cicero, Cassius, Casca and others; the tribunes
follow *'after'*. The expectation of the audience could scarcely be
greater, yet the episode is over in twenty-four lines. Extreme
economy is used: in a very few minutes two matters engage
attention and twenty-one speeches are heard.

Obviously Shakespeare is holding back, keeping the full display of Caesar and large action in reserve. But on the other hand
nothing seems hurried or scamped. There are four incomplete
lines in the (mostly regular) iambic pentameters, each suggesting
a pause (lines 2, 5, 11 or 12, and 23); and after three of these it is
Caesar who breaks the silence, drawing the play forward. He
makes his points with absolute clarity, calling both Calphurnia
and Antony by their names twice over. He also calls twice for the
name of the unknown man who hails him, and asks twice that this
man should be brought into his presence; and he then twice
commands the soothsayer to repeat what he has already said –
and Caesar knows that he has said. Finally Caesar indicates twice
that the assembled company should go off stage to the Feast.
He had previously directed this departure, but had held back when
the Soothsayer called his name; on that earlier occasion he had
bidden that no 'ceremony' should be left out (11). The effect is
uncanny: here is confident brevity that can take its own time, and
yet there are repetitions; and there is no ostensible reason for
repeating anything.

The rhythms of this introductory passage, with many short
sentences and repeated words, are both forceful and unsustained.
Seven syntactically complete utterances have only one word each,
four or five have two words, and five have three. These alone
would serve to break up the decasyllabic basis of speech into
jumpy and assertive sound. The longest sentence is less than four
lines long (6 to 9); and that is divided after one and a half lines,
and has further adverbial and participial phrases that must

introduce slight pauses in delivery. The only verse-lines in this first
episode that run their full length without some kind of break are,
with one exception, all Caesar's: lines 3, 15 and 16. The last of
these is the only line where the sense flows on into the following
line: this is for Caesar's response to the 'shrill' cry of the Soothsayer that calls his own name unexpectedly. By his rhythms alone,
Caesar is shown to be in control; his rein is tight and response quick.

The exceptional line, consisting of a whole speech without a
break, belongs to Brutus: 'A soothsayer bids you beware the ides
of March' (19). This is his sole contribution to the episode and so
is doubly impressive; it is also a repetition of what all but Caesar
have already heard – and he, indeed, may be supposed to have
heard well enough. Moreover the metre is irregular so that it
should probably be spoken as prose or, possibly, as an Alexandrine;
or it could be roughly elided to fit the blank-verse norm: in any
of these ways it will stand out from its context by its metrical
contrasts as well as by its sustained phrasing. Above all, this
exceptionally fluent response to Caesar is from an unnamed – and
therefore unknown – character making his only contribution to
this episode, and played by one of the star actors of the company:
attention is bound to be paid to this reiteration. Again there is
something uncanny here: the audience knows Caesar is to be
killed, and *he* does not: perhaps this speaker shares the audience's
knowledge; perhaps the audience will (rightly) guess that he will
be the killer. The short, broken rhythms of every speaker except
Caesar are counterstated at the point of menace.

Caesar dominates this first episode by what he is as well as what
will become of him. He is placed at the centre of a crowded picture, and he is the most, indeed the only, persistent speaker: every
other speech is his. He initiates every topic and action, so that all
the other words in the episode, except the first call of the Soothsayer, are spoken in direct response to what he has just said; and,
of course, the menacing Soothsayer is there and intervenes because of what Caesar will become. All the interesting words and
the single metaphor belong to Caesar: there is no image, pun or
unusual or idiosyncratic word in all the other speeches put to-

gether. Yet the strange thing is that the context which he so thoroughly dominates is full of interest, giving an impression of variety, pressure and division on all sides, as well as of dependence. There are six other speakers, each with an individual tone and pitch of voice. Only once is Caesar followed by the same speaker for two successive speeches, and that is early on when Antony is called to his presence. Moreover this impression of variety is still further heightened in that some speeches are calls, meant to be heard over background noise and music, or from a distance, and others are simple, man-to-man questions and answers. There are impressive silences too: Marullus and Flavius have, in the previous scene, been established as actively hostile to Caesar, and here the Folio directs that they should enter '*after*' Caesar's official party, and remain on stage without a word of comment until the general exeunt. (Later, at line 279, the audience is told that at the Lupercal ceremonies Caesar orders them 'to be put to silence'.) Calphurnia is silent too after Caesar, her husband, has spoken to her, a contrast to the ready response of others within his circle. When Caesar and his train leave, to a flourish of trumpets, Brutus and Cassius remain behind; these two, independent refusals to conform to a general movement will draw strong attention, especially since there has been no verbal preparation for either individual act.

In this presentation, Caesar himself will feed a questioning or suspicious awareness. His address to his wife at first sounds capricious and, more particularly, his 'directly' (3) may seem to give unnecessary precision. Then, without a reply, he calls 'Antony' and a young and nearly naked man, carrying a whip, will step obediently forward. The Folio stage-direction insists that Antony enters '*for the course*', and in Plutarch's *Lives* Shakespeare had read that on the Feast of Lupercal:

> there are divers noblemen's sons, young men ... which run naked through the city, striking in sport them they meet in their way with leather thongs, hair and all on, to make them give place. . . . Antonius, who was Consul at that time, was one of them that ran this holy course.

And many noblewomen and gentlewomen also go of purpose to
stand in their way, and do put forth their hands to be stricken . . .
persuading themselves that, being with child, they shall have good
delivery; and so, being barren, that it will make them to con-
ceive with child.

Shakespeare's change from 'holy course' to 'holy chase' in
Caesar's subsequent explanation, gives an indication of how he
imagined the Emperor's mind going; his 'touched' for 'stricken'
further suggests a tenderness or reserve; and, more clearly, the
introduction of 'Shake off their sterile curse' adds a sense of
struggle and of fated ill-fortune. When we try to appreciate what
happens on stage in the first ten lines, it helps to consult Plutarch
and this, in itself, is interesting; it indicates that Shakespeare chose
to give an inexplicability to this episode, a sense of action going
forward that is only partially explained or supported by the
words. Calphurnia is asked to 'stand' as if the course involved her
alone, and the purpose of doing so is not explained until afterwards. There are ironies too, for, while Caesar acknowledges a
'sterile curse' on his own account, he explains his request with
'our elders say' (7) as if in excuse for his superstition. When Antony replies, he adds 'When Caesar says, "Do this", it is performed' (10) which (ironically) attests Caesar's authority in a
business in which Caesar is clearly impotent. Antony, merely
by standing ready for the race beside the older and infirm Caesar,
will also draw attention to the oddity of dealing with such a
private matter in so public a manner; perhaps Caesar's 'Set on,
and leave no ceremony out' is an attempt to generalize his
personal need for involvement in the Feast of purification and
fertility.

The other business that is raised in this first appearance of
Caesar in the play is puzzling in another way: the deliberate and
repeated commands to ensure that he sees and hears the man
whose 'shrill' voice has spoken over the tumult are followed by
a rapid judgement and dismissal: 'He is a dreamer, let us leave
him. Pass' (24). Dreams, like 'curses', were matters of superstition,
and highly personal in implication, and so personal issues and

contradictions within Caesar are once more manifested; but they
are not explored or even written large. Of course the actor of
Caesar will have studied his part as a whole and so be able to give
credible reality to these adumbrations of drama to follow. He
will know that Act II, Scene ii shows Caesar responsive to dreams,
and that Cassius reports in II. i that Caesar

> is superstitious grown of late,
> Quite from the main opinion he held once
> Of fantasy, or dreams, and ceremonies.   (195–7)

And everyone in this first episode will know that Caesar will
appear as a Ghost before the battle of the last Act, and that
Brutus before his death will acknowledge:

> O Julius Caesar, thou art mighty yet;
> Thy spirit walks abroad, and turns our swords
> In our own proper entrails.   (V. iii. 94–6)

The conclusion of the drama, with the full manifestation of
animosities and inner tensions, and with the working-out of
prophecies, dreams and curses, is all implicit in this early episode.
Shakespeare's introductory strategy is to keep them implicit
only, so that the whole fabric of private and public life, including
speech, silence, physical presence and the inter-relations of men
and women, is all brought under scrutiny before the main issues
are clarified. The plot concerns large-scale events of rule and ambition, but by this handling of the drama they are realized with
meticulous and questioning attention to the detail of individual
engagements.

Brutus and Cassius, remaining on stage, use at first the earlier
manner of ostentatious simplicity: 'Will you go see' . . . 'Not I' . . .
'I pray you do' (25–7). But Brutus introduces more elaborate
language in order to be sarcastic at Antony's expense: 'gamesome'
(28) meaning ready for the race *and* (trivially) playful; and 'quick'
(29) meaning lively *and* quick to obey. After this, his reassumed
public manner to Cassius, with a metrical stress on '*your* desires',
sounds more personally involved in trust, more directly acknowledging that every man has his own business and desire. Cassius

shows that he has caught the implied confidence by deflecting the talk away from public affairs to a judgement about 'show' of personal love and acceptance. A confrontation between two men, beginning with an explicit acknowledgement that they have hidden their thoughts from each other, now follows to offset the public start to the scene.

The phrasing of speech lengthens. Verse-lines flow smoothly, the sense running over from one line to another on several occasions. At the same time, there is greater freedom for explanatory or qualifying parentheses. Images are now more common, and repetitions serve to deepen or define more clearly a thought that is reluctantly uttered, or hard to express. The longer speeches gather rhythmic strength towards a climactic statement at their close, as in lines 46-7 and 59-62.

Yet while the audience will readily, and probably with relief, follow the more sustained dramatic line of this duologue, they are not given a simple dramatic issue immediately. While the two men move towards mutual understanding, they become ever more clearly two very different people. Brutus speaks straight away about deception; his imagery changes from a 'veil' (37), to 'soil' or staining (42), and then on to 'war' (46), so giving a progressive impression of a struggle that becomes more general as its expression becomes more direct. His mind is restless, moving from one word to another to describe his inward consciousness: from 'trouble' (38) to 'passions of some difference' (40), and then to 'conceptions' (41) which in this sequence seems to emphasize what will happen rather than what is now realized; he then acknowledges forgetfulness through the 'war' within himself. All this time he is contrasting 'shows' (47) or 'behaviours' (42) with an inward reality in which 'love' is assumed to live in spite of outward 'neglect' and inward struggle. Clearly if his 'friend' can be 'deceived' (37), he himself is not settled in what he says when he asks for trust, nor in how he sees himself.

Cassius is the first to talk of a 'show of love' (34) but, when Brutus has used a variation of this phrase at line 47, he at once takes the idea further with a new image of 'mirrors' (56) and 'shadow' (58), or image as opposed to reality. This complicates the explicit concern with what is hidden and also shows how Cassius plays upon the man he talks to. In his first reply he had taken the image of physical exploits from Brutus's sarcastic account of the 'gamesome' Antony, and converted it from running to horsemanship, in order to imply that Brutus controls his friend like an unruly steed – when in reality he is ready to be a responsive mount. Yet this oblique challenge is so handled that Cassius here seems intent on appearing blunt and open with the concluding 'your friend that loves you'. Probably the audience will not be aware of the irony when Brutus replies, with apparently equal openness: 'Cassius, Be not deceived' (35-6), but the actor of Cassius will know that at the end of their talk together he has a soliloquy in which to acknowledge that his aim has been to 'seduce' Brutus (306), to 'humour' (309) and deceive him. Cassius is watching, waiting, soothing and trapping his 'friend', from the beginning; indeed he has stayed behind for this purpose, and his words give an actor scope to show this indirectly.

Cassius's reply to his victim's first long speech answers the images of 'soil' and 'war' with 'buried' (49), and 'conceptions' with 'Thoughts of great value, worthy cogitations' (50). Then Cassius asks a simple-seeming question, not hiding the fact that he is about to draw his 'friend' out further: 'Tell me good Brutus, can you see your face?' The trust he aims at is to be based on the recognition of deception and hidden motivations. He uses flattery, answering 'poor Brutus' with 'Brutus' (48) and then 'good Brutus' (51), and later with 'noble Brutus' (62). As he draws towards his point in this avowedly personal confrontation, he brings other witnesses to testify – 'many of the best respect in Rome' (59) – for his purpose is not in fact a gesture of personal trust, but political action. He is still quick to keep a watch on Brutus, accepting Brutus's awareness of 'strife', but converting it to a 'groaning underneath this age's yoke' (61).

Brutus is now ready to listen, and his question about 'dangers' suggests that he has accepted the political opportunities at which

Cassius has only hinted. The crux of understanding is probably in the three words 'Except immortal Caesar' (60). This can be nicely judged in performance, for the words may be given or, more subtly, refused an ironic intonation: Cassius is even at this moment planning to assassinate the 'immortal' of whom he deferentially speaks. Moreover it is at this point that Cassius, probably after a pause indicated by the incomplete verse-line, deflects the talk by delaying the personal issue of involvement; so he will draw further political commitment from Brutus.

The mixture of personal and political concerns in this duologue is closely contrived. It starts in the manner of the earlier public talk, and some characteristics of that continue, in the pauses at lines 31 and 54, and in the short-phrased, unsubtle 'I'll leave you' (31), 'Be not deceived' (37), 'be you one' (44), 'can you see your face? No Cassius' (51-2), ''Tis just' (54), and worked in as the completion of a much longer sentence, 'had his eyes'. The use of proper names is far more frequent than merely friendly conversation would require, and echoes Caesar's manner from the earlier episode, especially when Brutus talks of himself as 'Brutus' (46). Yet even while the two men are ostensibly talking together about personal trust and politics, and are using (and developing) each other's words and images, they are also both expressing individual tastes, preferences, unconscious biases. For example in talking of struggles and difficulties, Cassius uses images of oppression: a rider and a horse, burying, groaning under a yoke; he seems to expect aggression. In contrast, Brutus uses imagery of contest: games, civil war, differences, a leading into danger; he seems to expect a call for action. Brutus has the firmer rhythms when concluding a speech; although his willingness to listen to Cassius is phrased as a question, it runs through two and a half lines with scarcely more than a single break at the end of the first line; he speaks of the unknown and is facing up to Cassius's 'seduction', and yet he retains strength, which seems all the stronger by immediate contrast with the broken rhythms which prepare for Cassius's most direct approach.

Individual involvement on the deepest levels of consciousness and the interpenetration of political and private issues become abundantly clear in performance. An actor speaking the last lines given to Brutus in this passage will discover in rehearsal that his contrasting rhythms provide a means of defining and so strengthening his role. He will mark the connections, the common associations, between a sequence of images used in varied contexts, because this will give him consistency and a useful guide to unspoken emotional and physical reactions. He will know when Cassius must follow his lead, and when he must himself move quickly to hold some part of the audience's attention that is following Cassius. He will note all the changes of initiative, the hesitations, ambiguities, rhythmic climaxes, tensions arising from difficulties of expression and from sudden clarifications. His task is always more than simply realizing and then communicating the sense of what he has to speak, for the actor is present on stage and must attune his whole and continuous performance, his movements and various attitudes of attention, to the reality of his conscious and unconscious being as described *and* suggested by the words he speaks.

So the duologue, in performance, becomes the total activity of two men, expressing not only the line of argument, but also the changes in levels of awareness or points of contact between them, the points of balance between various movements, the dynamism and shape of the encounter. In Shakespeare's dramatic dialogue, the actors will find innumerable hints for inward and outward, physical, emotional and intellectual, performances. So the silence after Brutus has moved ahead with the word 'dangers', and before Cassius is ready with his next response, may have a larger and more absorbing theatrical reality than any moment when only one of the characters is speaking; the changing balance of the encounter is a source of theatrical excitement as the hidden, the unconscious and unknown, psychological bases of their beings become evident. This is not to say that the inward drama is as immediately comprehensible or as memorable as the drama that is fully defined and conveyed by words as they are spoken, but that, in this first Act of *Julius Caesar*, Shakespeare has

ensured that the main forces of his drama are at work at various
levels of accessibility to the audience. At this stage of the drama,
the audience is shown a world alive within and between men,
unresolved and capable of change and fulfilment.

Act III, Scene i

CAESAR: I could be well moved, if I were as you;
  If I could pray to move, prayers would move me.
  But I am constant as the northern star, 60
  Of whose true-fixed and resting quality
  There is no fellow in the firmament.
  The skies are painted with unnumbered sparks,
  They are all fire, and every one doth shine;
  But there's but one in all doth hold his place. 65
  So in the world; 'tis furnished well with men,
  And men are flesh and blood, and apprehensive;
  Yet in the number I do know but one
  That unassailable holds on his rank,
  Unshaked of motion; and that I am he, 70
  Let me a little show it, even in this,
  That I was constant Cimber should be banished,
  And constant do remain to keep him so.
CINNA: O Caesar –
CAESAR: Hence! Wilt thou lift up Olympus?
DECIUS: Great Caesar –
CAESAR: Doth not Brutus bootless kneel? 75
CASCA: Speak hands for me!   *They stab Caesar*
CAESAR: Et tu Brute? – Then fall Caesar!   *Dies*
CINNA: Liberty! Freedom! Tyranny is dead.
  Run hence, proclaim, cry it about the streets.
CASSIUS: Some to the common pulpits, and cry out, 80
  'Liberty, freedom, and enfranchisement!'
BRUTUS: People and senators, be not affrighted.
  Fly not, stand still. Ambition's debt is paid.
CASCA: Go to the pulpit Brutus.
DECIUS: And Cassius too.
BRUTUS: Where's Publius? 85

CINNA: Here, quite confounded with this mutiny.
METELLUS: Stand fast together, lest some friend of Caesar's
    Should chance –
BRUTUS: Talk not of standing. Publius, good cheer;
    There is no harm intended to your person,   90
    Nor to no Roman else. So tell them Publius.
CASSIUS: And leave us Publius, lest that the people
    Rushing on us should do your age some mischief.
BRUTUS: Do so; and let no man abide this deed,
    But we the doers.

Enter TREBONIUS

CASSIUS: Where is Antony?   95
TREBONIUS: Fled to his house amazed.
    Men, wives, and children stare, cry out, and run,
    As it were doomsday.
BRUTUS: Fates, we will know your pleasures.
    That we shall die we know; 'tis but the time,
    And drawing days out, that men stand upon.   100
CASCA: Why he that cuts off twenty years of life
    Cuts off so many years of fearing death.
BRUTUS: Grant that, and then is death a benefit;
    So are we Caesar's friends, that have abridged
    His time of fearing death. Stoop Romans, stoop,   105
    And let us bathe our hands in Caesar's blood
    Up to the elbows, and besmear our swords;
    Then walk we forth, even to the market place,
    And waving our red weapons o'er our heads,
    Let's all cry, 'Peace, freedom, and liberty!'   110
CASSIUS: Stoop then, and wash. How many ages hence
    Shall this our lofty scene be acted over
    In states unborn and accents yet unknown.
BRUTUS: How many times shall Caesar bleed in sport,
    That now on Pompey's basis lies along,   115
    No worthier than the dust.
CASSIUS: So oft as that shall be,
    So often shall the knot of us be called
    The men that gave their country liberty.
DECIUS: What, shall we forth?

CASSIUS: Ay, every man away.
Brutus shall lead, and we will grace his heels   120
With the most boldest and best hearts of Rome.

Enter a SERVANT

BRUTUS: Soft, who comes here? A friend of Antony's.
SERVANT; Thus Brutus, did my master bid me kneel;
Thus did Mark Antony bid me fall down,
And being prostrate thus he bade me say: 125
Brutus is noble, wise, valiant, and honest;
Caesar was mighty, bold, royal, and loving . . .

After scenes of dispute and conference – about Caesar's triumph, his refusal of the crown, the action needed to stop his acceptance of it, various responses to omens, dreams and the decisions of others – Shakespeare here sets action at the centre of the dramatic illusion. Until now a thunderstorm has been the noisiest, most violent occurrence. Portia, wife of Brutus, had given herself a 'voluntary wound . . . in the thigh' (II. i. 300–1), but she did this off stage and mentions her action only eight lines before she exits. The audience's attention has been directed towards argument, verbal statements and shifting or obscure motivations, but now the focus is on the killing of Julius Caesar: on a crowded stage there is a moment when 'hands speak' (76) unequivocally.

The verbal drama of this passage is significantly different in style from that of the earlier one examined. Caesar holds the centre of attention before he is killed, as in his first appearance before the Feast of Lupercal, but now with an elaborate speech that seeks to still opposition to his will; this is not successful, and he is forced to interrupt the next two petitioners while they sustain the dramatic development. He is then, abruptly, stabbed, as the audience expects and he does not. Thereafter no single character dominates the talk: at one point Brutus seems to lead, but Cassius soon takes over, and when Decius asks for action it is Cassius who takes charge, though asking Brutus to 'lead' (120). Then all is held up for an anonymous Servant who enters without preparation or identification.

In what is said there are few sharp transitions of mood or subject that are originated within the mind of the speaker: Trebonius deflecting talk from Antony to the crowd of Romans (between lines 96 and 97), Brutus changing from talk of Caesar's death to suggest that the conspirators should 'bathe' their hands in 'Caesar's blood' (105), and Cassius pausing to consider the effect of their actions on future times (at line 111), are the most noticeable moments when the talk could not be wholly foreseen by the audience from what has been said before or from what has happened. After the death of Caesar, this scene, in contrast to earlier ones, is chiefly actuated by what happens: the need to justify the murder to the people and to quieten the rapidly spreading alarm, the need to check where everyone is and to pay immediate attention to Trebonius and the Servant on their entries. Here events, not thoughts, are seen to be in charge; speakers do not progressively reveal the full nature of their involvement in a situation but are forced to reveal it sharply and briefly, by actions as much as by words. The focus is wider than any individual's consciousness: attention is sustained by events, and directed to individuals only in relation to these events.

Shakespeare's skill is here most evident in the way in which the stage picture is made meaningful, and each action defined and strengthened by contrast with others. At the start of the episode Caesar sits at the centre of the assembled Senate (see lines 31–2 and 34) and, beginning with Metellus, the conspirators all kneel to him in turn (see lines 36, 43 and 56); the repeated gesture is held to give cumulative effect, for twenty lines after he first addressed Caesar, Brutus is still 'kneeling' (75). When these suppliants rise it is to kill: and then Caesar himself 'falls' (77). In the following scene Antony describes what happened: when Caesar saw Brutus stab him:

> Ingratitude, more strong than traitors' arms,
> Quite vanquished him. Then burst his mighty heart;
> And in his mantle muffling up his face,
> Even at the base of Pompey's statue,
> Which all the while ran blood, great Caesar fell.
>
> (III. ii. 182–6)

E

This later account and Caesar's last words (line 77) suggest that Shakespeare had Plutarch's account in mind:

> Men report also that Caesar did still defend himself against the rest, running every way with his body. But when he saw Brutus with his sword drawn in his hand, then he pulled his gown over his head and made no more resistance.

A multiple killing (that leaves Caesar's mantle full of gashes), a recognition, and then a hooded figure falling: these are the essential and strongly contrasted elements of the action. The dead figure lies at the 'basis' (115), or plinth, of a monument to Pompey, his adversary in civil war. The tables have been neatly and completely turned from the moment when Cassius had petitioned, 'As low as to thy foot doth Cassius fall' (56), or when Caesar had asked if Cinna wished to 'lift up Olympus', the mountain home of the gods.

The next action clearly establishes the fear which is aroused as the conspirators gain initiative. The 'people and senators' (82) fly from the scene, and some of the conspirators start to run off too to proclaim their success. So, after the formal supplications and the moment of death, the stage is alive with action and cries, for which 'mutiny' is Cinna's word (86). At this point Shakespeare contrasts the isolated figure of Publius. Brutus first calls for him, and probably a pause follows as he is searched out, for the verse-line (85) is not completed. When he is found the audience, with the contributors, will turn attention on this aged senator. He is unmoving and silent, 'quite confounded'. Metellus seems to catch fear from him and, probably with drawn sword, calls for a stand to be made against an enemy. Brutus quickly silences his fellow-conspirator and, quite ineffectually, calls for Publius to be of 'good cheer' (89). But the mischief is done; his reassurances evoke no response, and even the implied request that Publius should leave is ignored. Shakespeare holds the dramatic focus on this paralysed figure still longer, as Cassius tries to get him to leave for the sake of his own safety, and Brutus briefly follows suit. The text does not make clear when Publius at last makes his exit; probably he does not do so until attention is deflected by the entry

of Trebonius, and Cassius's immediate enquiry about Antony,
whom Trebonius had earlier drawn away from the Capitol
(see line 26). Everything has been held back by the panic-
stricken Publius, with whom the conspirators are powerless, as
he with them. Shakespeare has made a physical detail dominate
the stage and provide an exposure of isolation, helplessness and fear.

News of Antony is quickly given, but what Trebonius chiefly
speaks of is a more general fear and so relates immediate concerns
for the first time to a general apprehension, to recognition of
'doomsday'. Line 96 is another incomplete verse-line, and this,
together with the repeated expression of fear, suggests that this
moment brings a quieter understanding: certainly it is followed
by a new mood. Brutus now apostrophizes the 'Fates' (98), and
Casca joins him in a reflection on mortality and acceptance of
death. Shakespeare does not develop this theme with long speeches:
the change of awareness leads to new action as Brutus asks for a
rite of concerted identification:

> Stoop Romans, stoop,
> And let us bathe our hands in Caesar's blood
> Up to the elbows . . .   (105–7)

Again the conspirators bend or kneel before Caesar; and Cassius
points the significance of this action by repeating Brutus's word
'Stoop' (111). As they crowd round the dead body, probably in a
tight 'knot' (117) that hides both it and their own faces, all except
the two leaders are silent: and, of course, the corpse can make no
reaction as Caesar had done. When the deliberate action is complete, Decius calls 'What, shall we forth?' (119) and on this line,
or just before, everyone on stage, except the dead man, will face
outwards with blood-covered hands and weapons: they are
revealed anew as a 'savage spectacle' (223), 'bloody and cruel'
(165) as Brutus later acknowledges. Now, however, words
counterpoint the spectacle; Brutus, who had initiated the action,
is silent, and Cassius gives the necessary instruction:

> Ay, every man away.
> Brutus shall lead, and we will grace his heels
> With the most boldest and best hearts of Rome.   (121)

The killers assume grace, courage and heartfelt virtue: words and visual effect are in sharp contrast.

As the newly ordered group is about to move off there is an unexpected disturbance and Brutus calls, 'Soft, who comes here?' and then identifies a 'friend of Antony's'. Again Shakespeare focuses the drama on an almost unknown figure, whose manner is in contrast to that of the conspirators. Almost certainly he, like Publius, is afraid, and he acts before he speaks; the difference here is that he does what he has been told: – 'kneel', 'fall down', be 'prostrate' – and then he speaks (123–5). The technique of providing a series of visual and physical images that are both like *and* unlike each other, here achieves a complex clarity. Not merely does one figure now kneel to the conspirators, as they had knelt to Caesar, but Brutus is picked out from the conspirators to be honoured as Caesar had been among the Senate: the audience will look at Brutus as much as at the Servant, and the nature of leadership and subservience will be expressed in the spectacle of the carefully speaking messenger and the red-handed leader. The messenger's speech gathers energy with two catalogues of virtues that bring Caesar sharply back to the audience's consciousness:

> Brutus is noble, wise, valiant, and honest;
> Caesar was mighty, bold, royal, and loving . . .

The audience has been brought to a simultaneous awareness of the effects of the murder on men's hopes and fears, and on their words.

While action drives this episode forward and the juxtaposition of actual, physical images supplies clarity and strength of effect, the words, at the same time, continually sharpen and widen the audience's consciousness. In part this comes from echoes that words awaken from other, earlier scenes. The most persuasive are those aroused at the very beginning by Caesar's identification of himself with the 'true-fixed', 'northern star' ruling in the 'firmament' (60–2), 'unshaked of motion' (70). In this self-assessment may be heard foreboding memories of the storm scene, when Casca had said that 'all the sway of earth shakes like a thing unfirm' (I. iii. 3–4), and that the tempest seemed to be 'dropping fire' (10). Under the 'disturbed sky' (39), men had been afraid and trembled (see line 54), and Cassius alone was prepared to 'tempt the heavens' (53). If Caesar's words define the position he assumes by awaking contrasting echoes of this disorderly storm, so, in the outcry that follows his murder and his fall from central power, the talk of 'mutiny', fear, amazement and 'doomsday' (86, 82, 96 and 97) are like earlier reactions to the 'civil strife in heaven' (I. iii. 11), the portents of 'fear and warning Unto some monstrous state' (70–1); here as the actors portray fear, both actions and words carry the same echo.

When the conspirators bathe their hands in Caesar's blood there is an echo of Calphurnia's dream that Caesar had retold in Act II, Scene ii (76–82), saying that in consequence of this his wife had begged him ('on her knee', line 81) to stay at home:

> She dreamt tonight she saw my statue,
> Which like a fountain with an hundred spouts
> Did run pure blood; and many lusty Romans
> Came smiling, and did bathe their hands in it.

Not only is the verb 'bathe' used in both instances, but the description and enactment of what was earlier only described is an actual fulfilment of the earlier prophecy.

Many echoes are more uncertain in their effect, although the reactions of some characters who had used the words earlier or the actors' awareness of self-quotation may make them more apparent in performance than in reading. When Caesar says he is '*Unshaked* of motion' (70), Cassius might be seen to remember how he had told Brutus earlier, with repetition, that 'this god did *shake*' (I. ii. 121), and how his soliloquy after this duologue ended with the lines:

> And after this let Caesar seat him sure,
> For we will *shake* him or worse days endure. (315–16)

Cassius is not in the centre of the picture at this time, and has been silent for twelve lines: but Caesar might look at him, and so direct passing attention, for he knows Cassius to be 'dangerous' (I. ii. 195) and Cassius is the last man to speak to him before this long speech.

Some echoes are not verbally precise, but none the less effective by a development from the earlier usage. When Brutus asks his followers to bathe their hands in Caesar's blood, his words in juxtaposing 'friends' and 'blood' (104 and 106) come close to those he had used to argue against killing Antony with Caesar,

> Our course will seem too bloody, Caius Cassius,
> To cut the head off, and then hack the limbs . . .
> Let us be sacrificers, but not butchers, Caius. . . .
> O that we then could come by Caesar's spirit,
> And not dismember Caesar! But alas,
> *Caesar must bleed* for it. And *gentle friends,*
> Let's kill him boldly, but not wrathfully;
> Let's carve him as a dish fit for the gods,
> Not hew him as a carcass fit for hounds . . .
>
> (II. i. 162–83)

The actor will mark the change between plan and actuality, between seriousness of forethought and seriousness of the act, with its obvious consequences of fear and misunderstanding. When Cassius considers how often actors will impersonate their deeds, he may awaken an echo of Brutus's exhortation at the end of the same scene of preparation:

> Let not our looks put on our purposes,
> But bear it as our Roman Actors do,
> With untired spirits and formal constancy . . .
>
> (II. i. 225–7)

Certainly Brutus is quick to pick up the theatrical reference, but this time the thought carries him back to reality, to the now senseless and ignominious corpse of his 'friend'. He does not speak again until the servant enters, and it may be that he is silenced by his thoughts, no longer finding comfort in the idea of mere performance; Cassius comes in quickly with a more positive note:

> So oft as that shall be,
> So often shall the knot of us be called
> The men that gave their country liberty.   (116–18)

While the echo of an earlier scene suggests that Brutus is shown expressing thoughts beyond his first intentions, and revealing a tendency (that will become clearer in later scenes) to be held back by thoughts of what the killing of Caesar has done to his hopes and fears, this episode does not dwell upon this, nor develop it beyond a brief moment: the dramatic focus is kept wide, and emphasizes the effect of actions rather than the development of individual feeling.

Such effects are nicely judged, and are of great importance to the unity of the play. Action has not displaced psychological and verbal drama: rather, it has temporarily assumed the controlling influence. Within the physical and visual effects, and together with the excitements of hurrying events, Shakespeare has kept precise hold, by verbal acuity, on individual involvement. Actors seeking a 'through-line' for their parts will find precise guidance here and a number of difficult changes of reaction to effect; for them the drama is not suddenly simple, but suddenly more concentrated, and they must work with special care and energy to create performances that can carry them through this scene without falsehood or jarring detail. To consider the verbal life of this episode, stage by stage, is to reveal the magnitude and subtlety of its challenge to its stage interpreters.

The basic verbal style is close to that of the earlier episode that we have examined. There is little descriptive or allusive imagery, few puns, and the vocabulary is for the most part simple – nowhere more so than when Brutus and Casca talk of facing death (see lines 98–102). Again Caesar has more complex imagery than the others, and this introduces strong words such as *fire, hold, flesh, blood*. Considerable repetition is used by the various speakers, but in differing manners. Caesar's speech is carefully controlled by repetition, his 'moved' and 'move' in the first two lines being neatly summed up in 'motion' of line 70, his 'one' of line 65 being picked up at the end of the comparison at line 68, and 'hold' one line later; 'constant' of line 60, that introduces the basic image of the 'northern star', is repeated twice in the concluding two lines when Caesar's generalization is firmly applied to the particular case in question.

The conspirators, however, use repetition like repeated blows with the same hammer, not as a structure or sustained argument; in their far shorter speeches words of activity and panic recur several times, as *run, proclaim, cry, fly, stand, stoop, forth*; for a few speeches after Trebonius's account of the people in the streets, there is repetition of *die, time, days, years, death*, simple words used without apparent development or gathering strength. The conspirators occasionally use repetition with more conscious effect, but not to shape an argument like Caesar; for them, some words become slogans: 'Liberty! Freedom! Tyranny is dead' (78), is the first statement immediately after Caesar's death; this is changed significantly in two repetitions, with 'enfranchisement!' (81) and then 'Peace' (110) instead of 'Tyranny'; finally the slogan is reduced to 'liberty' as Cassius uses the word to particular purpose in describing the conspirators with bloodied hands and swords (118).

With simple vocabulary and revealing repetition, the predominantly short-phrased rhythms of Act I, Scene ii are also used again in this passage. Less than one in ten lines flow on from one iambic pentameter to the next. Only Caesar has a preponderance of decasyllabic lines that run their full length without a break; many lines have three or more breaks. There is also the same tendency to use strong, syntactically complete phrases of one, two, three or four syllables only, and this is apparent in Caesar's sustained speech as well as, more obviously, in others. In the conspirators' slogans, the short phrases, mostly of single words, follow on each other in groups of three and so have an almost mechanical insistence not found in the earlier passage.

There is a further development of the device of repetition in the last two lines of the Servant's that are quoted here; he uses adjectives where very few have been used before, and he follows one decasyllabic line of four units with another of almost identical pattern; and these are prepared for by a three times repeated 'thus' and 'bid me' (or 'bade me'). Especially when heard in relation to the verbal style of the passage as a whole, this messenger will gain careful attention, will sound wary, firm and insinuating all at once; he establishes a new rhythm, a new density of utterance, with which to introduce a concentrated and ambiguous account of those personal qualities for which the main characters of the play are repeatedly and variously assessed. So Shakespeare begins to turn from the drama of events to that of character, and uses words that echo from previous scenes and will become increasingly significant in the last scenes where Cassius and Brutus face death themselves. These carefully balanced catalogues are ironically and noticeably placed: their rhythms (almost in step), the spectacle (one apprehensive servant prostrate before the blood-stained, purposeful 'friends' of Caesar), the verbal juxtapositions (of Brutus and Caesar, 'loving' and 'honest'), all set the audience's mind on edge, even in the midst of stirring activity; they prepare for the apparent simplicity and colossal ambiguity of Antony's final words over the dead Brutus: 'This was a man' (V. v. 75).

Shakespeare's care for individual psychological reality underlying this scene of action is best appreciated by following each individual in turn.

Caesar is at first in command, both cold ('*northern* star') and shining with 'fire' (60 and 64). He uses the first person singular to lead and control his thought. Yet there are two off-centre suggestions in his language. The more obvious is the false modesty, 'let me a little show it' (71), that mocks his hearers with a hint that he needs their permission – at once counterstated by the sharper rhythm of 'even in this' (71). Immediately before this, not so explicit, is the other counter-suggestion: it is implicit in an aggressive allusion to warfare that assumes a conflict which is denied in the main celestial image: one 'That unassailable holds on his rank' (69). The word 'unassailable' occurs nowhere else in Shakespeare's plays, but 'assail' does, and has clear military connotations; so the word 'rank' is here clearly a pun, meaning position both in society and in lines of battle (as often in Shakespeare).

When Caesar's expostulation and veiled hostility does not silence his petitioners, he shifts his position: first he tries an absurd comparison, speaking of lifting a mountain, so presenting himself as inhuman in the double sense of godlike and insentient; but then in sharp conflict he argues from a particular human case, noting among all the senate the kneeling figure of Brutus. His death speeches, both short, stress in the gripping focus of an end to resistance the same two opposing selves: the personal relationship of trust in Brutus and the 'fall' of a commanding figure. The fact that Latin is used for.the address to his 'friend' gives a wholly unique emphasis to this reaction: it must stand out, a moment that shifts the nature of the audience's attention to give an immutable point of historical 'reality' and of dramatic contrivance. Shakespeare's use of words at this still centre of the action shows his concern with Caesar to be grounded in an ambiguous, questioning view of the personal basis of trust and political power.

The minor characters show a sharply defined variety of individual response. Cinna is alert, but after being the first to notice Publius he takes no individualized part in subsequent events; he fizzles out. Trebonius, although charged with a particular responsibility towards Antony, moves, possibly after a pause, to recount with the particularized image of 'stare' how fear and judgement have possessed the people: no one else makes this transition, or is specifically aware of these considerations. Decius is the eager conspirator, withstanding Caesar's sharp command 'Hence' to Cinna, correcting Casca with 'And Cassius too' (84), and breaking through the ritual of blood-smearing with 'What, shall we forth?' (120): he is practical and unreflecting. Casca is 'blunt', true to his nature as expressed and defined in Act I, Scene ii, but without his accustomed edge of humorous detail. Metellus is ready for defence, being the first to fear for the consequences of their actions on themselves; but he stops, or is stopped by Brutus, half way through his alarm. For much of the scene the individual conspirators act together; but they are carefully defined individuals that must be realized independently if their words are to ring true in utterance; each will have his own rhythm, his own concerns; and each will have a changing reaction to the events.

Brutus, in the first reactions to the assassination, is the first to be concerned with the senators, and with Publius in particular. He is the first to check Metellus, and directly and soberly to accept the consequences as a 'doer'. He takes his next line from Trebonius, accepting 'doomsday' for himself, and for his fellow-conspirators; his mind takes span of his whole life, and all men's lives even in the danger and excitement of the moment of action. From this, in general terms, he reconsiders Caesar's death, and names himself with others as Caesar's 'friend' (104): for an actor this moment will probably suggest a sharp memory of Caesar's 'Et tu Brute', for this far more precise claim directs Brutus's attention back to the body and leads him to suggest that 'Romans' should 'stoop' (not 'fall') and identify themselves with their 'deed' in gruesome particularity (compare line 94). After this act, in which Brutus is closely identified with all the other conspirators, it is he who talks for the first – and indeed only – time of 'Peace' (110), significantly rephrasing the slogan of achievement. It is perhaps noticeable that Brutus uses the epithet 'red' rather than 'bloody' for their 'weapons' and that he insists that they should wave them 'o'er' their heads: after the act of identification comes a new distancing from the occasion itself; his mind, perhaps, seeks escape. However, when Cassius speaks of future times, Brutus in contrast moves back to his dead 'friend' and relates him to other victories and to 'dust' (116). His mind is unquiet, as Caesar's was, torn not merely between personal concerns and political need, but also by the need to know himself and accept consequences. He is the first to notice Antony's messenger, and with 'Soft' (122) stills the enthusiasm of the moment to hear him; his recognition is, significantly, of a *friend* of Antony's', a word now charged with double, troubling value.

Cassius is, at first, the practical man, dealing with immediate problems and future strategy. The major puzzle of his involvement in the scene is his introduction of the notion of future theatrical representation of their actions: does he see Brutus's ritual as merely theatrical? does he realize the political advantage of such a routine? It is perhaps indicative of this implicit understanding that when he accedes to Decius's suggestion that they go 'forth' into the streets he puts Brutus in physical command – at the moment that he assumes direction himself – and that he calls, not for performance but for bold 'hearts', focusing on the centre of affection and trust. For him, the greeting that Antony's messenger brings will echo his thoughts, or at least those thoughts that he has just made public.

In this episode of *Julius Caesar* Shakespeare's dramatic style has superb assurance, not only handling the larger events with economy and lively narrative interest, but also defining the activity of every one of the *dramatis personae* with deft precision.

When directors and actors work on this text in rehearsal, they discover those opportunities that serve their own needs, predispositions and abilities to enact. There are so many hidden directions in the printed text that usually only a few of them are followed in any one production. Sometimes Brutus dominates, sometimes Cassius; sometimes Caesar is conscious of the ambiguity of his speech, at other times he is the dupe of circumstance or his own egotism. Some productions hold the focus upon Publius so that the effect of his paralysis is inescapable, others use this episode as a vehicle for showing the divided counsels of the conspirators. And so on. So much is missed in each production that Shakespeare's style may be mistakenly judged permissive, rather than abundantly alive, consciously ambiguous, and capable of portraying characters in speech and action at several levels of consciousness.

In seeking to read the printed text, the first task is to ask as many questions as possible and to realize the theatrical accompaniments of the words; the second is to begin the slow building-up of a complex awareness and to allow the many small perceptions to interact upon each other. At this stage of study, our first, simple and often exciting 'reading' will be exchanged for fragmentary impressions, doubts and, sometimes, mere ingenuity. The time has then come to wait, and after an interval to re-read without asking specific questions or seeking definition; in this way we may find, if we are lucky as well as industrious, that the details come alive again. The inner unity of the writing, the single creative imagination of Shakespeare's mind, may begin to be recognized and to give abundantly assured life, proportion and inter-relationship to the whole complex creation. Precise and detailed work, patience, imagination, ease and good luck, are all required for appreciating Shakespeare's dramatic style.

The task is endless. For one thing, Shakespeare's imagination outstrips our own. But even without this obvious barrier, we should expect an alternation between assurance and perplexity in this study. If we had discovered all the hidden clues to performance that were contained in the printed text, the next step would be to respond to the varying effect which is necessarily given to any enactment through the changing conditions of production.

As the audience changes and encourages the actors in differing ways, so performance changes. A small stage accentuates different qualities in a text from those revealed on a large stage; a cold auditorium gives its own basic rhythm; the topical political climate will give particular emphasis to certain words; the physical weight of an actor will make the rhythms and proportions of his performance unique, and so will his emotional make-up and intellectual history. When Shakespeare decided to write for the theatre, he chose a medium that is adventitious: its effects are always being modified by interpreters and context. He put his imaginative mind to work with elements of which only the word printed on the page remains unchanging – and he took no special steps to see that that was inviolate.

A production can be eccentric because it does not recognize the challenges of the text; but the more responsible a production is the more freely it can respond to the changing conditions of theatre performance, which reflect the variety and accidence in human life and the changing conditions of human society. As Shakespeare developed as an artist he gave more and more freedom – or free play – to his plays: *Julius Caesar* is both highly controlled *and* wide open to varying presentations.

4 Twelfth Night

THIS comedy is the jewel of Shakespeare's plays: compact and brilliant, formed with obvious and minute skill, and yet reflecting various and surprising lights according to the mood in which it is read or the conditions in which it is performed.

For a study of Shakespeare's dramatic style, *Twelfth Night* offers two special kinds of writing. The first extract considered here is the beginning of the play, a short scene that combines memorable lyric simplicity with intimations of dramatic conflict within and without the character presented. The second and third extracts show a conscious artistry in prose dialogue, where each speaker is sustained by an over-all verbal, rhythmic and rhetorical design; they also exemplify verse and song intermingling with prose, and Shakespeare's use of a corporate scene so that it leads to a climactic revelation of individual involvement.

In *Julius Caesar* no one could doubt the seriousness of the play's main theme or the acute intelligence with which it is handled. In *As You Like It*, the pastoral setting contrasted with a political background, the masque-like ending, and the sustained ironies deriving from Touchstone and Jaques, all combine to give a broad impressiveness to the comedy and engender a lively critical awareness in its audience. But in this later comedy, plot, action and incidents are all grounded on mistakings, and on the improbable interchangeability of twin brother and sister; its style has ease and agility. Both matter and manner could be held immune from critical investigation; and they can very easily escape, like air or water, from the grasp of elucidation. But this is, perhaps, one of the play's most remarkable achievements: in performance and in criticism the play needs the lightest touch and quickest perception, but if its humanity and imaginative range are to be realized the players and students must also contribute patience and careful consideration.

Act I, Scene i

Enter ORSINO, *Duke of Illyria,* CURIO *and other Lords;* [*Musicians*]

DUKE: If music be the food of love, play on,
Give me excess of it; that, surfeiting,
The appetite may sicken, and so die.
That strain again – it had a dying fall.
O, it came o'er my ear like the sweet sound   5
That breathes upon a bank of violets,
Stealing and giving odour. Enough, no more,
'Tis not so sweet now as it was before.
O spirit of love, how quick and fresh art thou,
That, notwithstanding thy capacity   10
Receiveth as the sea, nought enters there,
Of what validity and pitch soe'er,
But falls into abatement and low price,
Even in a minute; so full of shapes is fancy,
That it alone is high fantastical.   15
CURIO: Will you go hunt, my lord?
DUKE: What Curio?
CURIO: The hart.
DUKE: Why so I do, the noblest that I have.
O when mine eyes did see Olivia first,
Methought she purged the air of pestilence,   20
That instant was I turned into a hart,
And my desires, like fell and cruel hounds,
E'er since pursue me.

Enter VALENTINE

                          How now, what news from her?
VALENTINE: So please my lord, I might not be admitted,
But from her handmaid do return this answer: 25
The element itself, till seven years' heat,
Shall not behold her face at ample view;
But like a cloistress she will veiled walk,
And water once a day her chamber round
With eye-offending brine; all this to season   30

> A brother's dead love, which she would keep fresh
> And lasting, in her sad remembrance.
> DUKE: O she that hath a heart of that fine frame
> To pay this debt of love but to a brother,
> How will she love, when the rich golden shaft   35
> Hath killed the flock of all affections else
> That live in her; when liver, brain, and heart,
> These sovereign thrones, are all supplied and filled,
> Her sweet perfections, with one self king.
> Away before me to sweet beds of flowers: 40
> Love-thoughts lie rich when canopied with bowers.

> *Exeunt*

The sound of the first three lines, considered out of context, is sufficient to pose the problem of understanding. A speaker will tend to pause after the first line:

> If music be the food of love, play on, . . .

The fourth syllable is more lightly stressed than usual in Shakespeare's blank verse, so that the predominating vowels are the *u*, *oo* and *o*, and 'food' tends to command the line as a whole. The last two syllables are detached syntactically, and so both quicken and halt the line after the lower-toned eight syllables that precede as a single phrase. The light front vowels of the second line and its concluding polysyllable cause it to run more quickly; but the two breaks that are required by sense and syntax require a careful delivery, and prevent it from flowing too easily into the third line. Here front vowels continue and there is no pause until after the seventh syllable. This line and the two preceding ones are then all contained, given a finished shape, by the final three syllables: 'and so die'. A stress from the iambic metre comes on 'and'; then a back vowel, reminiscent of line one, returns unstressed with 'so'; and finally the monosyllabic 'die' introduces a new, stronger and distinctive vowel-sound, and completes the run of three lines. This verb, 'die', is syntactically linked with 'may sicken' immediately before, but sound, rhythm and metre tend to make it stand on its own as well as completing the utterance. Presumably silence follows, for the musicians must now

start playing again and the 'dying fall' to which Orsino next
alludes could scarcely come at the beginning of their music. So
after the smoothness of the long first phrase of line one, the
nimble detail of line two and the first part of three, the concluding
'and so die' has a light, deft, and decisive authority or command.

Of course, the meaning of the words and their dramatic import
must enter our investigation. The first line is introduced with
'If' and 'be', but then follow two assured imperatives: 'play' and
'give'. With the participle 'surfeiting', the speaker's involvement
has to change to reflection and consideration, and then to the less
assured 'may sicken'. After these verbs, the concluding 'die' in
association with 'so' and with its own decisive sound may well
seem decisive in meaning and effect as well.

Of course, the word 'love' in the very first line brings complex
problems. As always, its precise meaning must be defined by context and, as very frequently in Shakespeare, this is further obscured
because the Elizabethans did not use the word 'sex' in the same
ways as we do and 'love' often had to do duty for this word too.
In this passage, 'love's' implications are at first indicated by both
'music' and 'food', the one immaterial and fanciful, the other
physical, tangible and simple. It is the latter which leads on to the
succeeding concepts of over-eating, bilious disorder, 'appetite'
and ill health. However, these images do not strike the listener or
reader very directly because the latinate words – 'excess', 'surfeiting' and 'appetite'—with their lightness of sound and of
rhythm carry the mind easily onwards. It is instructive to put
Orsino's thoughts in words of other origins: then he might say
'make me spue with over-eating so that I no longer want to eat',
or 'make me sick of sex, so I no longer want sex'. To speak thus
would alter the music, implication and, even, meaning of his lines;
what such a translation demonstrates is that Orsino voices an
instinctive, sensuous response and an ugly thought with agility,
control and decisiveness. The music that is played – if it bears any
resemblance to the courtly music of Shakespeare's age – will add
to the refinement and control implicit in the manner of his speech,
and make the violence of his thought still less apparent to

twentieth-century ears. Associations of listening to 'classical' music
should be held together here with those of hungry sexual reverie.

That Shakespeare regarded the sentiments of these three lines
with an intellectual distrust or even distaste is clear from related
passages, especially those in the amatory poems. The hero of
Venus and Adonis reproves Venus with:

> Love's gentle spring doth always fresh remain:
> Lust's winter comes ere summer half be done.
> Love *surfeits* not: Lust like a *glutton dies.*
> Love is all truth: Lust full of forged lies.   (801–4)

In *Lucrece*, the narrator equates Tarquin's 'ill' venture in lust with
'the profit of excess' which

> Is but to surfeit, and such griefs sustain
> That they prove bankrupt in this poor-rich gain.
>
> (134–40)

Within the meaning of the opening lines of *Twelfth Night* is a
suggestion of lust, sexual fantasy, physical response and self-inter-
est, and of grief and pain. The rhythms of these lines are sustained,
and yet at first indulgent, and finally strictly contained. Their
sentiment is reflective, or even contemplative, and yet sharply
self-aware; Orsino is presented as capable of precise sophistication
and direct sensuous response.

The presentation of the character is paradoxical. Orsino asks
for satisfaction of an impulse according to a supposition; and then
quickens his utterance with the thought of killing the impulse that
gave rise to it. He seems to speak to his musicians and to the
attendant '*lords*' required by the initial stage-direction in the
Folio text; none of these speak to him as friend-to-friend and yet
he speaks to them of his most personal concerns as if in explanation of his orders. On both these accounts, the actor should give
an impression of secret involvement, unspoken pressures and,
even, of imbalance or tenseness; perhaps the most direct expression of this lies in the sharpening rhythms. But his speech is by no
means neurotic, for the full tide of the metre carries the thought
forward and the words never direct thought unequivocally to-

wards conflicts and oppositions. The first line, spoken by itself, seems both instinctive and without complication; and it stays in the memory strongly so that the following two lines – that in fact deny its healthful implications – seem to be safely held within its presence or influence.

In performance the three lines may be weighted in favour of elegance, self-concern, or naïveté; of intellectual uncertainty or intellectual witticism; of sexual frustration, irritability, or fantasy indulgence. The precise effect of each performance will depend on actors and directors, and on the control of the scene as a whole, and of the full five Acts.

The short scene can most easily be seen as a whole in terms of the physical activity that takes place, for that is soon described. Unusually for Shakespeare, the play begins with music, the characters being silent. When that music stops, the three lines are heard, and then the music begins again. Orsino alone has spoken, giving general orders that are silently obeyed. The audience may expect to wait until the music is again complete, and their preparing to do so will probably be accompanied by questions arising from the unfamiliar stage-technique: the audience *expects* words and is twice given harmonious music. Why? Who is this man? What will happen when the music is finished? Almost at once the music is stopped by another order from the same speaker. The audience then hears one particular falling cadence of music out of context, and at once the playing is stopped a second time. Now the musicians must relax their attention, pack up their instruments and music, and possibly leave the stage. All this is an enactment of a performance destroyed, quiet effort thwarted, expectations unsatisfied. Still no one else speaks, and Orsino now talks in general about the love that is the conscious centre of his motivation; this is probably in soliloquy and he may well move away from his attendants. Probably Orsino completes his thought so that there is now a silence, broken by Curio approaching to suggest other business, a distraction from the thoughts that so evidently disturb and render their speaker isolated and uncommunicative. But the distraction does not work; a pressure seems to be released in Orsino's blatant pun that leads back to his own feelings, this time expressed with 'fell and cruel' (22) animal imagery. By now Valentine has entered and is silent so that Orsino has to address him first. An answer is delivered that conveys Olivia's message in seven lines of careful verse and elaborate imagery. Its import is refusal, but Orsino does not complain or question its decree: paradoxically he seems almost pleased. First he praises Olivia and then imagines her in love, presumably with himself. He orders the lords to leave the stage before him, and he may well be alone for the last line, which follows the fantasy of 'sweet beds of flowers' with a generalized description of a lover's reverie that could be self-criticism or headlong indulgence. He leaves to follow his own lords.

The attendants are an important element in the stage-picture; they mark Orsino's isolation, silences and abrupt changes of mood. They mostly enter to listen, to say nothing, to go 'away' before him. Curio's proposal is ignored; Valentine's precise message achieves nothing, except a change of place and pursuit of new stimulus in flowers, beds, bowers and abundance. The activity of the scene as a whole is elegant, deferential, expansive, unappeased. There is no one to speak in criticism or contrast; all these elements are only implied. The audience must catch the implications for themselves, if at all; probably an awareness of imbalance or absurdity, helplessness or danger, is, at this stage of the play, only a fleeting impression. Orsino is in command, yet open to view: accessible and self-revealed.

Phrasing, metre and rhythms, as in the first three lines, reveal the energy of Orsino's mind, sustained and yet restless. Line 4 starts with a brisk order and almost equally brief explanation; then it lengthens easily into sensuous description in which sense overruns into two decasyllabic lines, only to be concluded with a sharp antithesis that commences its own verse-line: 'Stealing and giving odour' (7). Instinctive indulgence is here sharpened by intellectual awareness; the rhythms revert to quick, contained energy. The new line is completed still more briskly with two two-syllabled orders in quick succession – 'Enough, no more' – a verbally simple contrast. Then the apostrophe to the 'spirit of love' follows and is developed through seven complete lines. Yet no one phrase extends unbroken beyond a single decasyllabic unit. The control of thought is obvious, and coupled nouns of almost identical meaning – 'validity and pitch', and 'abatement and low price' – give self-conscious elaboration and iterative rhythm. The metrically irregular line fourteen – 'Even in a minute; so full of shapes is fancy' – must either be spoken with much elision or with a metrical break before the second half so that two successive verse-lines are incomplete. After this exceptional irregularity, the concluding line is regular, with a brisk polysyllable at the end, three intensitives – 'full', 'alone', and 'high' – and emphatic alliteration on 'full', 'fancy' and 'fantastical'.

Seeing himself as victim of his own desires, Orsino has three lines that run unbroken; but when he speaks directly of his suffering the iambic pentameters are twice broken and the shorter rhythms accentuated by a double epithet:

> And my desires, like fell and cruel hounds,
> E'er since pursue me. (21–2)

The adverbial beginning of the second line with 'E'er since' helps to maintain an emphatic rhythm to the conclusion. Orsino's one phrase that extends over three lines occurs in response to Olivia's refusal of his suit; but this is preceded by the short and simple 'How will she love' (35) and followed by the rhythmic repetitions of catalogue and parentheses:

> when liver, brain, and heart,
> These sovereign thrones, are all supplied and filled,
> Her sweet perfections, with one self king. (37–9)

The rhythmic variations of this passage suggest that Orsino's mind is impelling his feelings and utterance along; or else that the energy of his feelings is pressing forward, rejecting the first fluent expression and urging his mind to quick and emphatic thought.

While rhythm expresses the sustained energy of Orsino's mind, the complexity and depth of his involvement are shown by metaphor, simile and repetition of words and concepts in varying contexts. As in other plays about love - *Romeo*,[1] *Antony and Cleopatra* and *Troilus and Cressida* - ideas of life and death are frequent and paradoxically linked. Orsino wishes his appetite may 'die', and the music has a 'dying fall' (perhaps there are further linked ideas of conflict in 'strain' and 'came o'er'). The opposite idea is expressed in 'breathes' (6) and in 'quick and fresh' (alive and new), the epithets given to the 'spirit of love' (9); but quickly Orsino reverts to 'falls' and 'low' which stem from a comparison with the 'sea' in its obliterating, death-like capacity. This image of the destructive sea is sustained, but height and fullness return indirectly in '*full* of shapes' and '*high* fantastical' (14–15). Thinking of seeing Olivia 'first', life and death are expressed in a single phrase which adds both the immaterial 'air' and the corrupting and generally active 'pestilence' or plague – that insidious and corrupting stroke of death which nothing could resist and from which no one was exempt. This image also associates Olivia with a goddess, Diana, and Orsino with a hunter who pursues her in trespass of his true human state, as Actaeon who saw the naked goddess in the myth. Now the idea of death is accompanied with the trained ferocity of 'hounds' and the chase.

Valentine's message also alludes to life and death in describing how Olivia has vowed to hide herself from the life-giving sun in order to keep 'fresh' (the word echoes Orsino's earlier usage in line 9) a 'brother's *dead* love' (31). On this cue Orsino turns to the ancient myth of Cupid's arrows, the leaden one that wounds with disdain and aversion, and the golden one that wounds with love and attraction. But now there are other images of life: if Cupid's arrow 'kills' (36) other 'affections', those feelings are an abundant 'flock' and '*live* in her'. And now come images of kingship in 'sovereign thrones' and 'one self king', and of abundance in 'all supplied and filled' (38) and in the 'beds' and 'canopies' of flowers of the concluding couplet. Moreover the earlier commercial

[1] See pages 61 and 63, above.

imagery of payment and value, in the paradoxical 'stealing and giving' (7) and the negative 'abatement and low price' (13), now returns in positive assurance, introduced with 'pay this debt of love' and *'rich golden shaft'* (34–5) and crowned with 'love thoughts lie *rich'* of the last line.

The irony is that the images of life, kingship and wealth at the end of the scene are all associated with insubstantial 'thoughts': it is all supposition. The eating and animal images of lines 1–3 and 18–23 do find a kind of echo in 'liver, brain and heart' of line 38, which are at least anatomical; but these are not tangibly realized, quickly losing their bodily and personal qualities to become 'thrones' filled with 'sweet perfections'. Orsino moves between sexuality and idealization. This opposition is perhaps suggested by the very first phrase, in the linking of 'music' and 'food'; certainly it is evident in the change from 'spirit love' (9) to 'shapes', 'fancy' and 'fantastical' of lines 14–15. 'Fancy', for Shakespeare was a highly ambiguous word: in a crucial scene of *The Merchant of Venice*, it is mere outward attraction:

> It is engend'red in the eyes,
> With gazing fed; and fancy dies
> In the cradle where it lies.   (III. ii. 67–9)

In *As You Like It*, however, Silvius associates the 'power of fancy' with the wounds that 'love's keen arrows make' (III. v. 29–31), and in *All's Well* Helena follows – and in the end is rewarded for following – her 'idolatrous fancy' (I. i. 91). At the end of *Twelfth Night*, Orsino's last words hail Viola as his 'mistress and his fancy's queen' (V. i. 374). The restless energy of the rhythm, the changes, contrasts and paradoxes of the imagery and the ambiguity of the 'shapes', or illusions and varying appearances, of 'fancy', are all used by Shakespeare to portray the isolated, self-conscious, tormented and delighted Orsino, without once bringing him to rest in a single, clear statement of purpose and being.

The effect could easily become too confusing; as Feste tells him later:

> the tailor make thy doublet of changeable taffeta, for thy mind is

a very opal. I would have men of such constancy put to sea, that
their business might be every thing and their intent every
where . . .   (II. iv. 73–8)

But there is an important contrast within the scene, the recitation
of Olivia's message. Not only do metre, phrasing and rhythm
run clearly, but the elaborate images are nicely controlled, in
small compass reflecting many of Orsino's and adding references
to summer's heat and the passing of time, to tears and 'seasoning'
or preservation; here too, in 'cloistress', is the only reference to
piety, one of Shakespeare's most constant images for young and
enduring love. That Olivia's vow is unusual and unlikely to be
fulfilled is marked by an over-elaboration, especially in 'water
once a day her chamber round' (29), where word-order accentuates the absurd precision. But in context, as it is recited by
someone at two removes from the sender, the message will sound
controlled and regular. Such complicated balance is remote from
actual experience but is an appropriate spur to Orsino's thoughts.
More than this: as he listens intently, the speech provides both a
focus for the audience's interest in the narrative and a riddling
statement of many of the themes of this scene and of much of the
play.
    Again Shakespeare's art is unassertive, for no one on stage
responds to this strange message except with admiration and immediate excitement. Yet if Orsino pauses before he answers or,
better, if his words break with new and contrasting energy after
his attentive silence, there will be a moment in performance, in
the preparation for utterance, where the conscious centre of this
young man is observed to be secret, precarious and imaginatively
strong. The transition is expected in that its motivation and continuity of thought are obvious, but the manner of speech and the
quality of engagement are new. The dramatic style is basically
histrionic, in that the scene fully awakes only in acted reality.
    There is a further opportunity for a clear transition of mood,
possibly after a pause on the completion of one train of thought
with 'one self king' (39): here is a new decisiveness, an order,
'Away before me', followed at once by a renewal of sensuous

awareness. The exact effect will, again, depend on the staging of the scene as a whole and on the quality of realization and perform- ance given by the actor.

The first scene of *Twelfth Night* can establish two aspects of the one situation: isolation, indulgence, uncertainty, frustration and waste on one side; energy, openness of mind, danger and com- mand on the other.

Act II, Scene iii

Enter SIR TOBY *and* SIR ANDREW

SIR TOBY: Approach, Sir Andrew. Not to be a-bed after mid- night is to be up betimes; and 'diluculo surgere', thou know'st –

SIR ANDREW: Nay, by my troth, I know not; but I know, to be up late is to be up late.   4

SIR TOBY: A false conclusion. I hate it as an unfilled can. To be up after midnight and to go to bed then, is early; so that to go to bed after midnight is to go to bed betimes. Does not our life consist of the four elements?

SIR ANDREW: Faith, so they say, but I think it rather consists of eating and drinking.   10

SIR TOBY: Thou'rt a scholar; let us therefore eat and drink. Marian, I say, a stoup of wine!

Enter FESTE

SIR ANDREW: Here comes the fool, i' faith.

FESTE: How now, my hearts! Did you never see the picture of 'We Three'?   15

SIR TOBY: Welcome, ass. Now let's have a catch.

SIR ANDREW: By my troth, the fool has an excellent breath. I had rather than forty shillings I had such a leg, and so sweet a breath to sing, as the fool has. In sooth, thou wast in very gracious fooling last night when thou spokest of Pigrogromitus, of the Vapians passing the equinoctial of Queubus; 'twas very good, i' faith. I sent thee sixpence for thy leman – hadst it?

FESTE: I did impeticos thy gratillity; for Malvolio's nose is no

whipstock. My lady has a white hand, and the Myrmidons are
no bottle-ale houses.   25
SIR ANDREW: Excellent! Why, this is the best fooling, when all is
done. Now, a song.
SIR TOBY: Come on, there is sixpence for you. Let's have a song.
SIR ANDREW: There's a testril of me too; if one knight give a –
FESTE: Would you have a love-song, or a song of good life?
SIR TOBY: A love-song, a love-song.   31
SIR ANDREW: Ay, ay; I care not for good life.
FESTE: [*Sings*]

> O mistress mine, where are you roaming?
> O stay and hear, your true love's coming,
>   That can sing both high and low.
> Trip no further, pretty sweeting;
> Journeys end in lovers' meeting,
>   Every wise man's son doth know.

SIR ANDREW: Excellent good, i' faith.
SIR TOBY: Good, good.   40
FESTE: [*Sings*]

> What is love? 'Tis not hereafter;
> Present mirth hath present laughter;
>   What's to come is still unsure.
> In delay there lies no plenty,
> Then come kiss me, sweet and twenty;   45
>   Youth's a stuff will not endure.

SIR ANDREW: A mellifluous voice, as I am true knight.
SIR TOBY: A contagious breath.
SIR ANDREW: Very sweet and contagious, i' faith.   49
SIR TOBY: To hear by the nose, it is dulcet in contagion. But
shall we make the welkin dance indeed? Shall we rouse the
night-owl in a catch that will draw three souls out of one
weaver? Shall we do that?
SIR ANDREW: An you love me, let's do't. I am dog at catch.

In prose scenes Shakespeare often mirrored everyday Elizabethan
life with ingenious and topical detail. It is arguable that our comic
actors have the hardest task among those who try to make Shakespeare's language fully alive in performance today. From this

passage of *Twelfth Night*, for example, 'testril' of line 29 carries
references now almost wholly obscured by changes in the business
of living. Editorial glosses do not always help: '*testril*, sixpence'
most of them read, and so Sir Andrew seems merely to be echoing
Sir Toby with meaningless variation. Yet one point of the jest is
that 'testril' occurs only here in Shakespeare's plays, and that this
and a literary quotation from *The Athenaeum* of 1905 are the only
citations in the *Oxford English Dictionary*. Sir Andrew has probably
created a new word, a diminutive of 'teston', or 'tester', that was
used colloquially for 'sixpence'. More than this, a 'teston' was
actually a coin no longer in circulation, being withdrawn in 1548:
originally it was a shilling issued by Henry VIII, but it was subsequently debased and revalued at tenpence, ninepence and, then,
sixpence; those remaining in circulation unofficially were subsequently worth very much less. What then is the dramatic point
of Sir Andrew's newly-coined word? The strange form makes it
very much his own creation, so there is independence and, probably, pride in its use. As his next words specifically suggest, he is
determined to be both equal and different in comparison with
Sir Toby. He stands on his knighthood, so the old-fashioned
qualities of the word may also be significant: yet it is vulgar
parlance too, so that 'tester' is used only by Falstaff and Pistol in
2 Henry IV and *Merry Wives*.

   Clearly the encyclopaedias and dictionaries can provide clues
to the way in which such obscure words should be spoken, but
this is not the only way to revive their dramatic life. Even in such
topical detail, Shakespeare's imagination was working in a fully
theatrical way. Here, for example, the sequence of speeches and
interchange of 'lead' in dialogue further illuminate the jest and the
presentation of character. Since Feste's entrance, Sir Andrew has
been leading the talk until Sir Toby interjects, on line 28, with
'Come on, there is sixpence for you. Let's have a song.' This is
brisk and to the point, and so a contrast with Sir Andrew's
elaboration that immediately follows. It sounds as if Sir Andrew
has regained the lead, but Feste breaks into his speech (or, possibly,
fills in the pause as Sir Andrew runs out of words), with a specific

question, and it is Sir Toby who replies; Sir Andrew has now lost the lead. The effort at independence in 'testril' is submerged if not ignored: when he rises to talk again it is for eager agreement, and he repeats Sir Toby's sentiments and the Fool's words; only this time he is saying more than he knows: 'I care not for good life' (32). This speech is another self-assertion, but it is a riddle: does he care nothing for 'morality', or for the good things of life, or possibly, for life itself? Is this folly or recklessness, or an instinctive expression of bewilderment? Or, remembering the ability of fools to voice deep and strange truths, we may wonder whether Sir Andrew echoes (and retreats from) his own earlier thoughts about 'eating and drinking' (10), and so, in his wise folly, states the paradoxes of the Sermon on the Mount. In the Bishop's Bible, the version current in Shakespeare's day, the still familiar thoughts were expressed in words close to Sir Andrew's:

> Therefore I say vnto you, be not carefull for your lyfe, what ye shall eate, or drynke; nor yet for your body, what ye shall put on . . . Care not then for the morowe: for the morowe shall care for it selfe . . .   (ed. 1568: *Matt.* 6: 25–34)

Notice that Sir Andrew's riddle is placed climactically to close a string of repartee; it is the point to which a comic performer will instinctively work to make his main effect. Moreover a silence must follow while Feste prepares to sing, so that the paradoxes implicit in his foolish sally may reverberate in the minds of his listeners. When the song does come, it has plenty of matter in it to feed such thoughts – references to the end of 'journeys', to wisdom, folly and time, to 'present' joys, plenty and 'stuff' that 'will not endure'; and the music holds the drama still, without plot-development or activity, so that there is large scope for reflection and imaginative response.

As a jest, Sir Andrew's attempt at wit in the use of 'testril' is all the more effective as a contrast for his ensuing silence, and this in turn will make more remarkable his climactic and yet less obviously ambitious return to talk. If the actor has given a comical physical expression to the growing confidence of Sir Andrew

once he is in conversation with the Fool, the subsequent over-
riding of his contributions by Feste and Sir Toby, and his return to
talk with the quick rhythms of 'Ay, ay', will give suitable occasion
for comic variations of that physical performance: agitation and
delight; intimidation and collapse; renewed energy, waiting and
quick re-emergence. Then comes the more sustained rhythm and
distinct involvement of 'I care not for good life' which offers a
further variation: it may be offhand or glib, or sententious and
self-important, or puzzled, or perhaps even daring. It is the actor's
task to choose a concluding stroke of physical performance that
will use and sustain the rhythm of his text.

These comic prose scenes are eminently actable: in view of their
changing rhythms, their contrasting opportunities for physical
elaboration, their variation of lead and use of climax, it is arguable
that our comic actors have the easiest task in making Shakespeare's
dramatic writing alive in performance today.

The scene must be considered as a sequence of varying dramatic
activity; it was written for three comic actors whose professional
expertise could create striking physical performances, including
grimaces, strange walks and interpolated laughs, and who were
well able to 'speak more than was set down for them'. Proverbially,
we may say that a clown can make something of nothing.[1]

Consider the implications of the first three words: 'Approach,
Sir Andrew.' Two short phrases, a command and an identification,
give quickening rhythm: alliteration ensures flow and makes the
'Sir' stand out a little – an actor might be tempted to stress this
word in view of the play made with Sir Andrew's title here and
on the preceding entry (I. iii). 'Approach' implies that Sir Toby
enters first; perhaps Sir Andrew, who is clearly very conscious of
the lateness of the hour, stumbles on afterwards. Such a contrast,
with the quickening rhythm and possible sarcasm of the words,
provides two comic actors with the basis for gaining a laugh.
Certainly Sir Andrew enters silent and submits to indoctrination.

[1] See J. R. Brown, *Shakespeare's Plays in Performance* (1967), Chapter vii,
'Playing for Laughs'.

The Latin tag, 'diluculo surgere saluberrimum est' (to rise early
is most healthy), comes from a schoolboy's Latin grammar book,
and so we may guess that Sir Toby puts on a mock pedagogic
manner. He is stopped by Sir Andrew's simple answer that is
fully furnished with oath and emphatic repetitions; it starts with
shorter, more insistent rhythmic units than Sir Toby's. His conclusion is irrefutable, but Sir Toby denounces it with emphatic
ejaculation; and so the game-playing, with Sir Andrew the sober
top for the whip of Sir Toby's wit, is at once established.

'I hate it as an unfilled can' (5) may be intended to start a
sequence of comic business. A little later, at line 12, Sir Toby
clearly calls for a 'stoup of wine'; but when Maria enters she
brings only a reproof for their 'caterwauling' (66). At line 111, he
still calls for a 'stoup of wine'; but this time she replies with a plot
to gull Malvolio and leaves with 'For this night to bed, and dream
on the event' (160). Sir Toby now seems prepared for bed, but
he changes his mind and goes off stage to 'burn some sack' (174),
calling Sir Andrew once more to follow him. Throughout the
scene Sir Toby can act as a man seeking a drink, but taking various
other entertainments instead. If this is so, his comparison of an
'unfilled can' can betray his own interests in the middle of his
mockery of Sir Andrew. Then his return to Sir Andrew to spell
out his joke – and thus humorously to kill his own joke – can
sound like mock desperation or genuine weariness.

Now the joke is that Sir Toby's jest has run out, and he gets no
rise out of Sir Andrew. There are several laughs at this point: at
Sir Andrew still puzzling out the matter, or pretending to understand, or valiantly remaining unconvinced; at Sir Toby defeated
or, in an opposite reading, enjoying the spectacle of a completely
dense auditor. Then comes a surprise: a change of tack, and one
that shows Sir Toby expansive – perhaps still the pedagogue, but
prepared to discuss the very nature of human existence and the
variety of human response. Sir Andrew develops too: he no
longer says 'I know not' and 'I know', but 'so they say' and 'I
think it rather . . .' These phrases may be said with airy confidence;
but a slower, perhaps rather sly, sharing of a confidence, a tentative

expression of independence, may be more in line with the rest of the scene and characterization. Sir Toby's praise and eagerness for drink would be more effective in contrast with the latter interpretation: the mock 'lesson' would be over on good occasion – a 'filled can'; the master is pleased with his scholar, because he pleases himself.

Again Shakespeare provides a surprise, for Feste the fool enters, not Maria. We may expect Sir Toby to be looking out for Maria but, curiously, Sir Andrew sees him first. Possibly there is a pause as the thirsty man waits for his drink and then gives up in impatience; so Feste's entry a moment later would unexpectedly 'cheer' both the knights. This need not take very long: the quicker the pause, the more buoyant the comedy.

Feste claims their attention neither as master nor as pupil, but as an equal on the grounds of affection: but there's a challenge in his greeting (in the allusion to the picture of two fools, or two asses, with 'We three' as motto so that the viewer is the third ass). Toby responds with good fellowship and mockery, and asks for a song to be shared by them all. It looks as if the scene is to run away into corporate merry-making.

Sir Andrew is, however, the odd man out. After another of his petty oaths (he is famed for quarrelling and for cowardice; see I. iii. 26–9), he finds his voice in admiration and emulation. Does he remember accurately Feste's jests of the night before? Or is he striving for words about laziness ('*Pigro*gromitus'), vapidity ('*Vap*ians') and some sort of equator for a cube, or a queue? Either way the speech is sustained, in contrast to his shorter, conclusive contributions before the fool's entry; it has both longer phrases, and contrasting short phrases to give continued impetus. There is an access of loquacity and strength: Sir Andrew blossoms. Towards the end, the simple statement, ''twas very good' could provide a contrasting earnestness or tongue-tied honesty. The concluding remark claims complicity and also requests acknowledgement. While Sir Toby is revalued on Feste's entrance as fool in fools' company, Sir Andrew proceeds to reveal wonder, aspiration and a need for encouragement.

Feste now contributes in high style with comparison piled on comparison. Nothing is absolutely clear, and some editors are content to comment that the speech is 'probably mere nonsense' (*Signet Shakespeare*). In performance, certainly, the words should partly baffle, partly outclass Sir Andrew's stumbling echoes of earlier fooling; but they should also awaken a wide range of response, impertinent and intimate like much good fooling. We may paraphrase:

> I put the little tip that expressed gratitude in my long fool's petti-coat: Malvolio may smell out our fun but cannot punish with a whip – or (possibly, with an obscene connotation) if Malvolio is exposed there will be no punishment for anyone; – Olivia, my true mistress, is a gentle lady, a virgin; and we, merry-greek followers, have nothing to drink – or, are above vulgar, frothy drink.

It is a question whether Sir Andrew understands anything of this, except the sensation of being present at a great feast of fooling; he steps up Sir Toby's request for a catch to one for a song, in which the Fool will lead alone. And so we reach the interchange already examined in which Sir Andrew's happy excitement modulates to his own sort of natural nonsense, that may express good sense in an even more surprising way than the Fool's.

From the audience's point of view – watching what the actors do *and* how they do it – the interchange between speakers and the variety of mood and rhythm are as important as what the words precisely say. If the spoken text were all, there would be passages of both bewilderment and triviality; but in full performance these words can sometimes express fugitive and fantastic meanings, and sometimes contain within very simple form a wide relevance or questioning paradox.

The song is justly famous: simple monosyllables and fluent verse; varying polysyllables and full unbroken lines; contrast between feminine and masculine line-endings; proverbial formality and light intimacy; an easy and yet tactful flirtation between amatory and moral meaning; opportunities for singing 'both high and low',

according to sense and rhyme. There is a neat and climatically
placed allusion to fools with 'Every wise man's son', and a
thought-provoking repetition of the word 'present' at the crux
of the poem. Dramatically, Shakespeare delays the conclusive
'Then come kiss me' until after the 'unsure' has sounded but still
waits for its rhyme, and until the preponderance of negative
statements has been established. In performance, the song is like
an inset perspective within a larger picture: it shows great depth
in little compass; it holds back attention from larger dramatic
concerns. The image of life presented by the play is here both
vaster and more securely contained than in the lively dramatic
presentation of character, action, dialogue, spectacle.

Between the two stanzas Sir Andrew and Sir Toby stir only to
express satisfaction and (rare) unanimity. At the end of the song,
they praise, more specifically, the singing, and at once Sir Andrew
starts tripping into absurdity as he tries to cap the epithet 'contagious': Sir Toby meant a 'catchy song', but Sir Andrew, by
coupling it with 'sweet', awakens the senses of 'foul' and 'in-
fectious'. Sir Toby turns the word-play more surely to absurdity
and then calls for the catch to awaken the heavens, the 'night-owl'
and the timid, psalm-singing weaver. Agreement follows and
the Fool prepares to lead. In performance two actions are dominant here: now Sir Toby exerts himself fully in a progressively
exuberant invitation; and the three find they share a common purpose. Then there are two side-effects, the more subtle being the
silence of Feste after he has won approval: many opportunities
are provided in the play for Feste to stand aloof from his companions, to observe while others are totally involved. More
obviously, Sir Andrew shines in completely unaffected enthusiasm
and in anticipation of being 'dog at catch': there is no emulation
or self-consciousness, none of his customary oaths, in 'An you
love me, let's do't.' Even for this jubilant, shared moment,
Shakespeare keeps his characters distinct: each has a continuous,
subtextual, individual consciousness that gives life to the words
and to physical performance.

F

Act III, Scene iv

Enter OLIVIA *and* MARIA

OLIVIA: I have sent after him; he says he'll come.
How shall I feast him? What bestow of him?
For youth is bought more oft than begged or borrowed.
I speak too loud.
Where is Malvolio? He is sad and civil,   5
And suits well for a servant with my fortunes.
Where is Malvolio?
MARIA: He's coming, madam; but in a very strange manner. He
is sure possessed, madam.
OLIVIA: Why, what's the matter? Does he rave?   10
MARIA: No, madam, he does nothing but smile. Your ladyship
were best to have some guard about you if he come; for sure
the man is tainted in's wits.
OLIVIA: Go call him hither.

Enter MALVOLIO

I am as mad as he,
If sad and merry madness equal be.   15
How now, Malvolio?
MALVOLIO: Sweet lady, ho, ho.
OLIVIA: Smilest thou?
I sent for thee upon a sad occasion.
MALVOLIO: Sad, lady! I could be sad. This does make some
obstruction in the blood, this cross-gartering; but what of that?
If it please the eye of one, it is with me as the very true sonnet
is, 'Please one and please all'.   23
OLIVIA: Why, how dost thou, man? What is the matter with thee?
MALVOLIO: Not black in mind, though yellow in my legs. It did
come to his hands, and commands shall be executed. I think we
do know the sweet Roman hand.
OLIVIA: Wilt thou go to bed, Malvolio?
MALVOLIO: To bed? Ay, sweet heart, and I'll come to thee.
OLIVIA: God comfort thee! Why dost thou smile so, and kiss
thy hand so oft?   31

MARIA: How do you, Malvolio?

MALVOLIO: At your request? Yes, nightingales answer daws.

MARIA: Why appear you with this ridiculous boldness before my
lady?   35

MALVOLIO: 'Be not afraid of greatness'. 'Twas well writ.

OLIVIA: What meanest thou by that, Malvolio?

MALVOLIO: 'Some are born great' –

OLIVIA: Ha?

MALVOLIO: 'Some achieve greatness' –   40

OLIVIA: What sayest thou?

MALVOLIO: 'And some have greatness thrust upon them'.

OLIVIA: Heaven restore thee!

MALVOLIO: 'Remember who commended thy yellow stock-
ings' –   45

OLIVIA: 'Thy yellow stockings'?

MALVOLIO: 'And wished to see thee cross-gartered.'

OLIVIA: 'Cross-gartered'?

MALVOLIO: 'Go to, thou art made, if thou desirest to be so' –

OLIVIA: Am I 'made'?   50

MALVOLIO: 'If not, let me see thee a servant still.'

OLIVIA: Why, this is very midsummer madness.

Enter Servant

SERVANT: Madam, the young gentleman of the Count Orsino's
is returned. I could hardly entreat him back. He attends your
ladyship's pleasure.   55

OLIVIA: I'll come to him. [*Exit* Servant] Good Maria, let this
fellow be looked to. Where's my cousin Toby? Let some of
my people have a special care of him; I would not have him
miscarry for the half of my dowry.   59

Exeunt Olivia [*and* Maria]

MALVOLIO: O, ho, do you come near me now? No worse man
than Sir Toby to look to me? This concurs directly with the
letter: she sends him on purpose, that I may appear stubborn
to him; for she incites me to that in the letter. 'Cast thy humble
slough', says she. 'Be opposite with a kinsman, surly with
servants; let thy tongue tang with arguments of state; put
thyself into the trick of singularity'; and consequently sets down
the manner how; as, a sad face, a reverend carriage, a slow

tongue, in the habit of some sir of note, and so forth. I have
limed her; but it is Jove's doing, and Jove make me thankful.
And when she went away now, 'Let this fellow be looked to'.
'Fellow' not 'Malvolio', nor after my degree, but 'fellow'.
Why, every thing adheres together, that no dram of a scruple,
no scruple of a scruple, no obstacle, no incredulous or unsafe
circumstance – What can be said? Nothing that can be can
come between me and the full prospect of my hopes. Well,
Jove, not I, is the doer of this, and he is to be thanked.   76

This episode is clear verbally; hardly any glosses are required and
the sequence of thought is generally simple and immediately
comprehensible. But it shows Malvolio in love, is a turning point
in narrative and character-presentation, and is a favourite with
audiences and actors. For this Shakespeare has provided a clash
of performances, much physical business and a strong structure.

The basic clash is between what Olivia calls her own 'sad'
madness and the 'merry' madness of Malvolio (14–15); but the
two words seem more and more inapposite as the scene proceeds,
so that Malvolio becomes 'sad' and Olivia almost 'merry'. The
distinction that is progressively revealed is between a concern with
someone else and his ability to control one's life, and a concern
for one's self.

Shakespeare at first uses verse for Olivia in a quick, nervously
excited soliloquy that is immediately contrasted with an effort at
composure. She seems to enter ahead of Maria: the first verse-line
breaks after six syllables and her mind shoots forward to the
imaginary reality of Cesario's willingness to come to her – despite
his refusal ever to do so as he left the stage before (III. i. 155–60).
Only in the third line, when she rationalizes her impulsive questions, does the speech run the full decasyllabic unit; and at once
there is an abrupt, four-syllable line that checks her utterance, and
she turns to Maria. Now she manages an extended phrase with the
second line, but she relapses to a shorter phrase as she simply
repeats her first question.

Maria's reply starts with a brief sentence, but then her phrases
lengthen and the last is checked by a repeated 'madam'. She is

choosing her words and holding back her laughter. Olivia's response is surprisingly varied: questions that are neatly to the point; then a simple order; and finally, without more ado, a soliloquy that is quick and antithetical in which she associates herself with the strange news she has been told. The moment before she had wanted Malvolio because he was 'sad and civil'; now because he is mad. Olivia is trying to keep her head among conflicting emotions and perceptions. The very lightness of the concluding soliloquy of a line and a half, with its objectivity, its question, paradox, quick running rhythm and rhyme, suggests quick, excited movement and so accentuates her helplessness even as she momentarily gains control of her mind.

The Folio edition marks Malvolio's entry immediately after 'Go call him hither' (14), so it is likely that Olivia has seen the 'madman' before she talks of him. Possibly Shakespeare has engineered a surprise static moment: Maria turns to seek Malvolio; he, precisely then, enters; he says nothing, but perhaps smiles in the manner dictated by Maria's letter written in Olivia's hand and with which he probably left the stage in his previous scene (II. v. 158–9); no one speaks; Olivia turns aside for soliloquy. In such a confrontation all three would be helpless: Maria with suppressed laughter or delight; Malvolio with effort; Olivia with recognition: 'I am as mad as he'.

Whether Malvolio enters before or after the soliloquy, and whether or no Maria goes off stage to fetch him, on his entry he is silent and Olivia must speak first. Attention is thus directed to him; and yet the only words Shakespeare gives him are 'Sweet lady, ho, ho.' In performance they are quite sufficient, for the actor has much to do: he must have 'a sad face' and 'reverend carriage' (67); he must 'smile'; he must overcome his ability to 'be sad' (20) owing to the constriction of his cross-gartering; above all he must bring the reality of his dream of being 'Count Malvolio' (II. v. 30) and loved by all men and his mistress to the test of his acceptance. Clearly he has been let down before, as other people have failed to take him at his own valuation: when he first read the letter he had exclaimed, 'I do not now fool myself to let imagination jade me' (II. v. 145-6); it is this imagination he now has to live by. He is both excited and 'happy'; and probably his first silence shows that he is also, inwardly, afraid. Anyway, when the button is pressed by Olivia's concerned question, what at last pops out is pathetic – trite, vulgar or, possibly, tongue-tied. It is a moment for comedy or sympathy, or for objectivity; as often in Shakespeare, the kind of performance brought to the role will determine the effect of this climactic moment. The possibilities are endless: I have seen Malvolios trip up; I've seen them tremble, stutter, ogle, giggle or look transported with happiness; I have heard the words spoken blandly, quietly, loudly, sharply; Sir Laurence Olivier, at Stratford-upon-Avon in 1955, waved his fingers from behind a yew hedge, and disappeared again as suddenly as he had appeared.

At this point dialogue takes over and is clearly structured to show Malvolio's overwhelming self-concern, and weakness. It also shows Olivia's instinctive sympathy which, in its turn, holds the episode back from headlong comedy. The first correction from Olivia, 'I sent for thee upon a sad occasion' (19), is taken by Malvolio entirely with regard to himself, and so he fails even to ask his duty; the thought that he is overcoming inconvenience allows him to introduce his own satisfaction through the words of a common ballad. Direct personal questions lead to a riddle and then an attempted confidence which also shows his need for justification and assurance. This baffles Olivia completely, and so Shakespeare plays on the underlying sexual confusion directly in 'Wilt thou go to bed, Malvolio?' The victim hears this as a straightforward invitation, so that he calls his lady 'sweet heart' and promises to go to her bed. The odd – and comic – thing is that he does not seem to approach her at this point, but rather smiles and kisses his 'hand so oft' (31). He believes that Olivia offers herself to him, without matrimony; he accepts, and then puts off the encounter. He is again reduced to silence. Now he is so lost in his own thoughts that he does not hear Olivia's further questions, and Maria has to take up the challenge, repeating Olivia's simplest question: 'How do you, Malvolio?' (32). The physical exuberance suggested by the business described in the text, the misunderstanding, the need for Maria to intervene, all suggest that Malvolio is transported fully and excitedly into his imaginary world and is further than ever from being able to communicate with his lady: and that he is oblivious of this. This is comic, revealing and powerfully dramatic.

The surprise of Maria's question awakens Malvolio to some realization of what is actually happening. But when he re-emerges in dialogue he speaks wholly of himself, reciting the letter to his own satisfaction without hearing a word Olivia says. Neither her questions, her prayer to heaven, her frank incomprehension, nor her surprised reference to herself as 'made', 'maid' or, quite possibly, 'mad' (50), can stop the growing display of what 'love' means to Malvolio. The actor will find a physical performance to mark the progress of his ecstasy. At the end, Malvolio relates all to his own 'desire' and can even refer to his real role as 'servant' without in any way risking his complete satisfaction in an effusive expression of delight and pride. Olivia's last comment – 'this is very midsummer madness' – suggests that at last she realizes the sexual and licentious nature of his incredible fantasy. A rhythmic, physical and vocal climax in the actor's portrayal of Malvolio must have been reached here, sustained by his borrowed words, by the contrastingly short phrases of Olivia and, above all, by his complete isolation.

Shakespeare the dramatist intervenes at this point to introduce a servant to speak a brisk message. Perhaps this is doubly effective in that he seems unaware that anything strange is happening on stage; *his* mind is full of the recent and strange encounter with Cesario off stage in which he 'could hardly entreat him back'. Olivia settles on departure with speed, and it is noticeable that she sees Malvolio so completely wrapped up in himself that her concern for his safety is spoken wholly to Maria. Under the simple words with which Shakespeare directs the action forward, multiple energies and purposes are displayed: Maria has secret fun, especially as Sir Toby is introduced; Olivia is now decisive; possibly the Servant is relieved or expectant; Malvolio is still silent but now, once more, attentive – this is made clear as soon as he is alone on the stage, for he *has* heard every word.

The following soliloquy probably begins quietly, perhaps slowly: he may hammer out his renewed satisfaction, but with quiet, soft blows so that his security is not infringed. He has to pamper his assurance into a new bloom, only speaking when he has adjusted himself to what must seem the strange departure of his lady to seek out his rival. But by the time he starts quoting the vital letter a second time, he is probably swift and confident; the interjected phrases, 'she says', and 'and consequently', and the ensuing catalogue of 'a sad face, a reverend carriage . . .' invite a new liveliness of rhythm. It is then that he speaks a phrase that cuts through any pretence of love or service: 'I have limed her'. When he speaks thus directly and with notable imagery, he sees himself as catching a helpless bird: the satisfaction is with himself, wholly, and it is potentially cruel. He is not aware of anything odd in this, but proceeds to thank Jove for his good fortune: if he corrects his excited image of bird-snaring, it is only to deprecate his own cunning and so think of himself as favoured and loved of the gods. He can now remember her going 'away' (70), and translates the dismissive and perhaps contemptuous 'fellow' (56) into a term of affection. (When Laurence Olivier played the part he spoke the final 'fellow' very softly and protractedly, in luxurious self-indulgence.)

At this point, Shakespeare could have brought in Sir Toby, seeking Malvolio in accordance with Olivia's instruction; but he delays the necessary entry for two more revelations. First, Malvolio continues to speak of a 'scruple', or doubt, of his normal awareness of obstacles in his path and of what is 'incredulous' (or unbelievable) and 'unsafe' in his fantasy. Syntax is left incomplete as he realizes that he can now trust his new reality anywhere. He refers again to Jove but in contrasting manner to the previous occasion: now he is familiar with the god. Instead of 'but' to introduce the thought, it is 'Well'; instead of Jove being asked to make him 'thankful', there is an almost casual addition: 'and he is to be thanked'. An actor shaping this soliloquy will use the repetition and mark the contrasts clearly; and in doing this he will be led to show a further extension of Malvolio's response to Maria's practical joke. Malvolio has got 'what he wills', as the sub-title of the play puts it; and this is revealed progressively through dialogue, action and soliloquy.

Perhaps the most extraordinary feature of the dramatic style in this passage is Shakespeare's ability to make the clearest definitions of individual involvement seem to come instinctively, or naturally. But second to this is his ability to write dialogue that offers many open invitations to the actor – to provide verbal and physical opportunities which if followed with skill and ambition will shape the scene, control revelations of character, develop the audience's response in exciting and satisfying sequence. This is achieved without elaborate stage-directions and without the actor having to be wholly, or explicitly, conscious of what is afoot; an actor's instincts will guide him.

5 *Macbeth*

In *The Tragedy of Macbeth*, a study of Shakespeare's dramatic writing meets difficulties head-on. The most obvious is the condition of the text. There are few obvious cruces here and, by Jacobean standards, the original edition of the 1623 Folio was well set, with few misprints. The troublesome obscurities are mainly two-fold: first, the verse-lining is often irregular and, secondly, the punctuation frequently fails to clarify meaning or timing of utterance. The use of cast-off copy, with the subsequent need to fill out or compress the text on the printed page, is partly to blame, but so may be the condition of the manuscript from which the printer worked. This was probably a prompt-book that had been altered for court performance, or a transcript from such a copy. Simultaneous breaks in metre and sense look like signs of hasty cutting, and the shortness of the play – some 900 lines less than the usual Shakespeare tragedy – suggests that the cuts were extensive. But not all the textual difficulty can be blamed on the book-keeper in the theatre: there is, through much of the play, a compression of style that is appropriate to its theme and action, and this quality of the writing was probably the chief cause of the compositors' perplexity.

Indeed the greatest obstacle to an understanding of the text of this play is also its greatest achievement: a complicated interplay in allusion and ambiguity, an impression of rapidly shifting psychological pressures, and the interaction of sensuous response and intellectual activity. The tragedy centres on the characters of its two protagonists who are revealed to the audience in such a way that the innermost resources of their natures are progressively expressed, unconsciously and consciously, at the very moment of experience.

Macbeth and Lady Macbeth are roles that have attracted, and not infrequently defeated, the most ambitious actors of our theatres. Shakespeare was not confined by the limitations of those who first performed his plays, for history has shown that each actor capable of sustaining such a role has discovered fresh strands in the characterization, and that these alone have been sufficient to hold and transform his audiences. Both the main parts in this tragedy are superbly theatrical and finely sensitive characters: in following the text of these parts, it is necessary to respond as if one were capable of prodigious feats of physical and psychological performance. Neither Burbage and a boy-actor, who first played them, nor Albert Finney and Irene Worth, who may well be the most able to undertake them today, could be sure to answer the challenge at every turn. But this is one of the main justifications for a careful and thorough investigation of the dramatic qualities of Shakespeare's writing: losing the concentration and grip of a single performance, a theatrically conscious reader is able to lie in wait for the text to reveal still more of its potential, in one performance after another, in one exploratory reading after another. Over the years, moments of discovery – each bringing its own excitement – begin to cohere and give a developing sense of Shakespeare's imaginative conception: something of 'great constancy' that can so minutely control each detail of the writing and yet lie open to the changing emphasis of very different performances.

The passages chosen for consideration here are mostly concerned with Macbeth alone, so that they may effectively show something of the progression of character-portrayal. They are mostly soliloquy or the simplest forms of dialogue, so that attention is not deflected from the main problems of the play by the need to envisage complicated stage-business. They are also capable of varied consideration, corresponding to the three main types of study discussed in the Introduction to this book: the first passage will be approached through analysis of words, the second through analysis of action and spectacle, and the third through an attempt to foresee performance, to realize the demands made on the actor for a total presentation of the man.

Act I, Scene iii

MACBETH: [*Aside*]   Two truths are told
As happy prologues to the swelling act
Of the imperial theme. – I thank you gentlemen. –
[*Aside*] This supernatural soliciting   130
Cannot be ill, cannot be good.
If ill, why hath it given me earnest of success,
Commencing in a truth? I am Thane of Cawdor.
If good, why do I yield to that suggestion,
Whose horrid image doth unfix my hair,   135
And make my seated heart knock at my ribs,
Against the use of nature? Present fears
Are less than horrible imaginings.
My thought, whose murder yet is but fantastical,
Shakes so my single state of man, that function   140
Is smothered in surmise, and nothing is
But what is not.
BANQUO: Look how our partner's rapt.
MACBETH: [*Aside*] If chance will have me King, why chance may
   crown me
Without my stir.
BANQUO: New honours come upon him,
Like our strange garments, cleave not to their mould   145
But with the aid of use.
MACBETH: [*Aside*]   Come what come may,
Time and the hour runs through the roughest day.
BANQUO: Worthy Macbeth, we stay upon your leisure.
MACBETH: Give me your favour: my dull brain was wrought
With things forgotten. Kind gentlemen, your pains   150
Are registered where every day I turn
The leaf to read them. Let us toward the King.
[*To Banquo*] Think upon what hath chanced, and at more time,
The interim having weighed it, let us speak
Our free hearts each to other.
BANQUO: Very gladly.   155
MACBETH: Till then enough. – Come friends.
                                                    Exeunt

The contrary elements within the mind of Macbeth are shown by the verbs he uses – the actuating elements of his speech – and the nouns with their epithets, possessive phrases and so on. Most obviously, Anglo-Saxon monosyllables are contrasted with poly-syllables of Latin or Romance origins. The series of simple words contains the concepts *truths, ill, good; good, ill* and *truth* again repeated; and then physical objects: *hair, seated heart* and *ribs*. The other series of more elaborate words includes *happy prologues, imperial theme, supernatural soliciting, earnest of success, suggestion, horrid image*. The phrase *swelling act* (128) lies rather between these two series, being composed of simple elements, but combined in a polysyllabic phrase and referring, like the longer phrases, to a concept as well as a physical act.

The basic contrast is clearest in

> This supernatural soliciting
> Cannot be ill, cannot be good.   (130–1)

The simple words are large in reference but sharply opposed by means of repetition and antithesis. Indeed the monosyllables give no rest: the only fluency or ease in this passage as it is spoken comes with the lighter rhythms and more continuous phrasing of con-secutive polysyllables. At first the verbs draw attention only by repetition: *are told, can* and *be* (twice), *hath given*. But after *com-mencing* (133), which introduces the repeated *truth*, the verbs soon become sharply defined, active and haptic: *yield, unfix, knock*. This change comes after a short sentence in the present tense, making the simple factual comment: 'I *am* Thane of Cawdor.' From con-ceptual matters, expressed in both series of nouns and epithets, Macbeth turns to physical, for it is at this point that the simple nouns refer to his own body: *hair, heart, ribs*. There is perhaps a backward reference to 'swelling act' (128) which, in more general terms in the first sentence, had related concepts to deeds.

Part of the meaning of these first ten lines is defined by the sequence of individual words and their changing conjunctions. In the theatre, when these words are used as guides to perform-ance, the changing nature of Macbeth's engagement is given continuous physical embodiment, and contributes as much as individual sentences. The drama shows Macbeth wrestling with simple concepts and quick and complicated thought until he becomes aware of his present political situation in barest verbal terms that echo the witches' prophecies: after this moment of realization his whole physical being responds and he recognizes the sheer physical power of instinctive forces within himself.

At line 137, conceptual joins physical again, in 'use of nature', and now the simple and polysyllabic words take new conjunctions and oppositions: 'present fears' (137) refers to objects of dread, and this is followed by *horrible imaginings, fantastical, function* and *surmise*, contrasted with the simpler *thought, murder* and *single state of man*. Verbs in this almost wholly conceptual passage are both simple – *are* and *is* – and physical – *shakes* and *smothered*. The sense of actual engagement in palpable events and physical objects, introduced with 'unfixed' hair and 'knocking' heart, is now experienced in wholly imaginary thought. The conclusion of the first speech, marked by Macbeth's ensuing silence, uses once more the simplest elements of noun, pronoun, conjunction and verb:

> and nothing is
> But what is not.

But now the words, in themselves, are neither conceptual nor physical. They are antithetical once more; and once more – and overwhelmingly – negative: *nothing* and *not* affirm the reality of what has no present actual existence. Again Macbeth's performance gives an over-all and inescapable physical statement: linking his actual present condition with the future as he sees it in his imagination, he loses his present bearings and the ability to act; he is caught in an antithesis that represents both a concern for reality and a loss of it.

The speech first sharpens the antithesis of moral black and white. The use of 'ill' rather than 'bad' defines the opposition as between moral 'good and evil' (this was a common Elizabethan meaning of 'ill'), rather than between good and 'bad' fortune.

From this centre the energy springs, as can be seen in the changing rhythms of the whole. The phrasing here becomes shorter, repetitions giving insistence and a short, clear-cut rhythm: 'Cannot be ill, cannot be good.' The effect is continued in the brief 'If ill',[1] but the more conceptual phrase 'why hath it given me earnest of success,' gives renewed fluency. Then the present rings clearly: 'I am Thane of Cawdor,' but its metrical basis is not simple: *I* and *am* could both take a stress; the line as a whole has twelve syllables and possibly should be spoken as two half-lines, with a pause of realization between the two parts and after 'Cawdor'. The rhythms are here held in check, out of obvious balance, but after the phrase 'If good' which looks back in form to the earlier and opposing 'If ill', the rhythms are once more assured, and grow stronger and longer until the awareness of physical actuality comes firmly: 'And make my seated heart knock at my ribs, . . .' (136). The stress on 'knock' comes one syllable early, according with the active meaning of the verb. Lines 134–8 are the most regular in the whole speech: there is no run-over of sense from line to line, so that the metre gives a new impression of fitness and inevitable forward movement. With 'horrible imaginings', the rhythms are lighter, and then 'my thought', as a short phrase standing apart from its verb, is reminiscent of the beginnings of lines 132 and 134, and introduces the last long-phrased sentence. After a relative phrase, the verb 'Shakes' is strongly placed at the beginning of a line, and then the metre again becomes uncertain, the sentence continuing with explanatory, parallel phrases. Some editors mark line-endings, with the Folio text, after 'state of man' and 'surmise'; but at last the iambic beat – though not the full run of a pentameter – becomes unavoidably clear on:

> and nothing is
> But what is not.

[1] The text of the Players' Edition, quoted here, follows the Folio line-arrangement; some editors move 'If ill' to the end of line 131. One way it holds the rest of its own line in uneasy balance after a pause at the end of the eight-syllabled line 131; the other way, it forces line 131 to a regular conclusion and relates the fluently regular line 132 to the earlier, twice-broken pentameter.

In the changing references that words bring with them, the speech has a similar construction, but in this aspect it is more obvious that its beginning needs the ending before its full potential is realized. The first general reference is in the marked juxtaposition of 'ill' and 'good' in line 131, but Macbeth does not precisely consider anything outside his own predicament until 'use of nature' in line 137. At once he returns to himself, but now he is concerned with 'thought' itself. It is at this point that he changes from the vague 'that suggestion' and the more coloured 'horrible imaginings', to the bare word 'murder'. Until this moment Macbeth has considered but not named, not even in this soliloquy spoken to himself, the deed, the actual physical act which he foresees and realizes in his imagination. Even now the murder is not specified and will not be, directly, in the rest of the scene. Possibly the phrase 'single state of man' shows that Macbeth is thinking of kingship, and certainly the witches' message and the 'imperial theme' of line 129 place 'murder' in its full dramatic context and meaning; but the precise words are held back, 'Duncan' being avoided wholly, and 'King' being used later only for Macbeth himself, and as part of a pretended ease of manner in the direction, 'Let us toward the King' (l. 152).

The single sentence in the first speech that is not soliloquy – 'I thank you gentlemen' (129) – introduced after the first self-concerned sentence, makes some element of dissimulation absolutely obligatory at the outset of the soliloquy. (This is, we may suppose, the sole reason for its presence, for dramatic propriety or convenience cannot require it.) In performance, if its effect is to be clearly made, the words must contrast in tone, rhythm, pitch, volume and intention. So the brief sentence serves to mark both Macbeth's isolation and his ability to deceive at the very moment when, for the first time in the play, he takes and holds the audience's attention wholly for himself. Such a brief aside, so out of the main context of feeling, is normally a device for comedy, or for melodrama when the central character is a practised dissimulator, like Shakespeare's Richard III. The difference here is that while Macbeth dissimulates to others he is also dissimulating to himself in holding back the word 'murder', and is entering a world of uncertainty. He is not in control of himself, however much his aside shows him to be in control of others; in his mind are sharp antitheses posing doubts and fears, and, still more uncontrollable, an active, 'smothering' imagination that seems like reality.

That Macbeth's 'thought', as expressed by this soliloquy, carries him beyond an awareness of the present situation is revealed inescapably in performance as he changes from being able to give the brief, formal recognition of the 'gentlemen' to standing in silence, forgetful of everyone else. The dramatic effect is marked by Banquo who speaks of Macbeth at this point without addressing him; he describes his leader as 'rapt' (142) and links this with 'partner', a word that suggests he had expected to share his thoughts.

At the beginning of the soliloquy, Macbeth's words concern theatrical illusion, echoing those which Shakespeare had given to the Prologue of *Henry V*:

> O for a Muse of fire, that would ascend
> The brightest heaven of invention,
> A kingdom for a stage, princes to act,
> And monarchs to behold the swelling scene!

Macbeth's use of the image is elaborate and idiosyncratic: he is a man with a *double* cue to speak and act, and his stage is a world which is not yet realized in fact, and hardly in fantasy; a world of imperial rule and royal murder that is growing to active life in his own mind. After 'theme', he becomes conscious of an audience that is present too soon for the performance, and he acknowledges its presence in words that do not come from the drama he is so largely envisaging. When he next speaks for himself the image has changed, so that the two 'prologues' become secretive and personal: they are now 'soliciting'. And as he thus comes nearer to the reality that the witches have just activated within his mind, he recognizes both the 'supernatural' element and the moral conflict. Further responses now press to his attention: fear, doubt,

G

justification, hope; the train of action and reaction is set and conflict within and without begins. At the end of the soliloquy there
may be a return to a theatrical image: a sense of the falseness of
theatrical illusion, to set against its splendour, power and thematic
unity:

> nothing is
> But what is not.

(It is the trick of 'strong imagination' and the dramatic poet to
give to 'airy nothing' a 'local habitation and a name'.)

In reference and imagery the implications of this speech are
not easily measured, but the plain meaning of individual words is
in doubt only once, at a significant point after the naming of
'murder'. Although 'my single state of man' (140) sounds assured
and almost proverbial, it is this phrase that holds the annotators
in debate: does *single* mean 'solitary, alone, unaided' and, hence,
'weak' (as Steevens, Harbage, and Foakes believe), or 'individual'
(following G. K. Hunter), or 'indivisible', referring to the 'state
of man' as a 'little kingdom' as in *Julius Caesar*, II. i. 63–9 (as noted
by Grierson, Muir, Walter and others)? The context is complicated, including both 'fantastical' and the physically active
'Shakes'. The consciousness of Macbeth, as displayed in the speech
as a whole, could support all the proposed meanings and it could
well be argued that, for the moment, as he recognizes the overwhelming power of his imagination, he combines all these meanings in one phrase: he is alone, unique, and potentially monarch
over himself and over others. For all the forward movement
towards emphatic judgement and imaginary reality, the soliloquy
may also contain an astonishing self-awareness, almost a humorous detachment, near the point of climax.

Verbally there is still a further perspective. When Macbeth first
uses antithesis in speaking to and for himself, in 'Cannot be ill,
cannot be good' (131), he is distantly echoing his own speech at
the beginning of the scene which is also his very first in the whole
play: 'So foul and fair a day I have not seen' (I. ii. 38). Banquo,
who follows this brief speech, does not comment or reply, so it

may be a soliloquy, spoken for himself; if so, the echo that this in turn gives to the first scene of the play when the witches meet spectacularly in thunder and lightning to cry in chorus, 'Fair is foul, and foul is fair!' (I. i. 12), would be both more marked and more related to Macbeth's personal thoughts. When he attempts, in the present soliloquy, to control his thoughts and govern his deeds with moral judgement, he uses another antithesis, different in wording but closer in form to the witches' chorus: 'Cannot be ill, cannot be good'. He is entering the conceptual world of the witches, repeating something of his first instinctive response to the 'blasted heath' and the witches' unseen presence. They could be speaking through him; they could have foretold the way his mind would work. For the audience, a 'battle' may seem, at this moment, to be both 'lost' and 'won' (I. i. 4).

After Banquo's comment and his own silence, Macbeth has two more brief soliloquies. They are repetitive, not strongly antithetical. In the first, Macbeth makes all depend on 'If', 'chance' and 'why' and refers to himself passively; he dismisses his whole future activity as 'my stir', a physical word that echoes important elements of the preceding soliloquy, but in the shortest compass. At this he is again silent. The next speech is again highly repetitive: at first briefly, 'Come what come may', and then almost tautologically with 'Time and the hour'; it concludes with a rhyme that links 'day' back to 'may'. In this soliloquy there is again a physical element in 'runs' and 'roughest', but it is smoothed by alliteration and partly hidden by the rhyming conclusion and the dismissive implications of the whole speech. Shakespeare's tactic here is to keep the audience without specific verbal statement of Macbeth's intentions, even though he is speaking in soliloquy; and the repetitions make this the more noticeable by suggesting fluency of thought. The final couplet could be a dismissal of the consequences of his determination to kill Duncan, spoken as decisively as possible in order to still his own doubts: in this way the absence of reference to the 'imperial theme' and the generalizing nature of the words are an avoidance of earlier and now deeper thoughts. Certainly when he speaks aside to Banquo a few lines later, Macbeth is still concerned with future action rather than acceptance of 'chance', and is still looking for the appropriate 'time'. Or the couplet could imply that Macbeth intends to wait for 'chance' to fulfil the witches' prophecy and to endure his present frustrations and fearful imagination: so he would speak to Banquo, not with dissimulation on 'free hearts' (153), but in a plea for help and counsel. Or, again, Macbeth may be deceived by his own speech: he may intend passivity, or propose it to himself, yet inwardly be carried forward by his 'kindled' imagination (see line 121) that both horrifies and attracts, and is betrayed in the active and physical 'stir', 'run' and 'roughest'.

Certainly Macbeth is now able to be outwardly polite and careful, but the earlier soliloquy and the changing reactions that it implies are not wholly dismissed from his mind: he does eventually commit the murder and suffer for it, however successfully he convinces himself that he will abide the work of chance and time. His words are now remarkably simple, but *favour, forgotten, registered* and *interim* have something of the earlier polysyllabic complexity. Generally he picks monosyllables as if aiming at simple and bare statement, but it is in these that the physical element continues, in *dull, wrought, pains, turn, leaf, weighed*. Conceptually the backward links are clearest in echoes, many of which sound ironically against the earlier usage: so 'Think upon what hath chanced' (153) looks back to 'My thought . . . Shakes . . .' and 'If chance will have me King'. This speech, which is spoken aside to Banquo, may seem to be prompted by the conscious or unconscious echo provided by the preceding word 'King' (152), a reference to Duncan hitherto avoided. Other echoes of the soliloquies are 'every day' (151) that looks back to 'roughest day'; 'at more time' (153) that seems to contradict the acceptance of 'Time and the hour'; and, more obviously, 'things forgotten' (150), which instead of referring to routine matters as Macbeth's formality implies, refers back to 'nothing' and 'what is not', and the whole active and still unforgotten thoughts of the soliloquy.

The studied politeness, changing the earlier 'gentlemen' (129) to 'Kind gentlemen' (150) and, finally, to 'friends' (156), the rhythms that now lack any short, emphatic or rising elements, and the metrical regularity, all speak for a sustained control, and are all the more impressive for contrast with the charged irregularities of the main soliloquy. The subtextual energy, beneath the smooth deception of others and perhaps of himself, is manifest in the echoes, the reverberations of seemingly simple words, the abrupt speaking aside to Banquo and then, unmistakably, in the last line of all, with its short phrases and true contrasts: 'Till then enough. – Come friends.' On his *exit*, Macbeth is in command and seemingly free-hearted; but his words are once more abrupt, pressured from within his mind. It is noticeable in performance that neither Ross, nor Angus, nor Banquo answer him.

After the main soliloquy only Banquo speaks, and it is his brief words that heighten the impression of Macbeth's isolation and dissimulation, and that establish a counter-interest in the silent group that follows the new Thane of Cawdor off stage. Banquo's first words draw attention to the watchers, as well as to his presumptive 'partner' (142). His next contain an elaborate image that echoes words that Ross and Angus have already heard from Macbeth himself: 'Why do you dress me In borrowed robes?' (108–9); but for Banquo, they will also refer to the witches' prophecy: 'You shall be King' (see line 86). When he directly addresses Macbeth, he uses Ross's 'worthy' (106) and a deference that in 'leisure' denies the 'rapt' (or transported) thoughts he had marked to his other companions. With this dissimulating preparation, and in answer to Macbeth's dramatically ironic words, Banquo's concluding 'Very gladly', can hardly be received by the audience as a full expression of his thoughts. Macbeth's first comment on the witches' words after they had vanished had been 'Your children shall be kings': he does not now voice this rivalry, but it is possible that Banquo will strongly imply its presence.

The actor of Macbeth must choose how he speaks his last words: 'Till then enough. – Come friends.' Even if he says them lightly and easily, the impression they make as contrast to the deeply and variously charged soliloquy, to the apologetic formalities and the whispered aside, will focus the attention of the audience on what he does not say.

Act III, Scene iv

MACBETH: It will have blood; they say, 'Blood will have blood'.
   Stones have been known to move, and trees to speak.
   Augures and understood relations have
   By magot-pies and choughs and rooks brought forth   125
   The secret'st man of blood. What is the night?
LADY MACBETH; Almost at odds with morning, which is which.
MACBETH: How say'st thou, that Macduff denies his person
   At our great bidding?
LADY MACBETH: Did you send to him sir?
MACBETH: I hear it by the way; but I will send.   130
   There's not a one of them but in his house
   I keep a servant fee'd. I will tomorrow,
   And betimes I will, to the Weird Sisters.
   More shall they speak; for now I am bent to know
   By the worst means, the worst; for mine own good,   135
   All causes shall give way. I am in blood
   Stepped in so far, that should I wade no more,
   Returning were as tedious as go o'er.
   Strange things I have in head, that will to hand;
   Which must be acted ere they may be scanned.   140
LADY MACBETH: You lack the season of all natures, sleep.
MACBETH: Come, we'll to sleep. My strange and self-abuse
   Is the initiate fear, that wants hard use.
   We are yet but young in deed.   *Exeunt*

The dramatic life of this episode after the appearance of Banquo's ghost at Macbeth's banquet depends largely on two visual elements. The first is constant throughout – the sight of the stage after the guests have left on Lady Macbeth's urgent command:

   I pray you speak not; he grows worse and worse.
   Question enrages him. At once, good night.
   Stand not upon the order of your going,
   But go at once.

LENNOX: Good night, and better health
     Attend his Majesty.
     LADY MACBETH: A kind good night to all.   (117–21)

The table and its furnishings, food and drink, stools, the two chairs
of state, must all remain in place, in the disorder in which they
were so suddenly left. Macbeth and his wife, dressed for the
ceremonial feast as King and Queen, are left alone on stage.
Macbeth's cheek was 'blanched with fear' (116) when he encountered the ghost, as an object that could 'push' him from his
stool (82); after Ross's question 'What sights, my lord?' (116), he
has been silent; almost certainly he stands or sits, or has fallen,
some distance from the table and thrones. Lady Macbeth has
been in command and is therefore standing as the guests and
servants hurriedly leave; but when the stage-picture changes,
she does not speak. Two half-lines of verse suggest that with the
exeunt is a held silence, so that the spectacle can fully register on
the audience's senses.

The other visual effect now begins: the changing relationship
between the two remaining figures. As the audience waits for the
next word or the next move, attention will be intense. The last
effective contributions of Macbeth and his wife have been strongly
contrasted, and neither Macbeth's silence nor his wife's courteous
words could have expressed all that was in their minds. It is of
crucial importance who makes the first move in speech or gesture,
and Shakespeare has so arranged the following duologue that the
physical relationship of the two figures is maintained as a central
part of the drama.

Lady Macbeth could move first: she could sit, or turn to watch
where the last guest has gone; she could move towards her husband, or away from him. When she next speaks, her broken verse-
line with its falling rhythm, repetition, and image of chance or
balance, all suggest, in simple yet unforced reply to Macbeth's
question, a far different mental, emotional and physical involvement from that with which she bade her guests goodnight;
somewhere the change must have happened in terms of physical
performance, and the performer must choose where and how to

effect it, and whether the audience observes the change in several stages or registers it, with a shock, only when she speaks.

Shakespeare has given her no immediate verbal initiative, so the words of Macbeth will be the more effective if it is his voice, rather than a movement, that, quite quietly, breaks the held silence and stage-picture: 'It will have blood; they say, "Blood will have blood." ' The punctuation of this line is doubtful, the more so in that the Folio prints it as two half verse-lines; but since the proverb does not speak of 'It', the 'they say' needs to be linked to the second statement rather than the first; that is, the semi-colon should come after 'blood', not after 'say'. Between the two halves of the line there is a changed engagement, from a precisely foreseen consequence to a more general truth: this means that with speech some tension is immediately released. It is possible that for the second half of the line Macbeth could look at his wife, or else at the stage left in disorder after the feast, or out into space, or at the 'heavens' over the stage. His next three lines are a kind of catalogue, for which his mind must move quickly and precisely, involving another kind of response and physical attitude. The metre is regular; and after the first line, the sense runs from one verse-line into the next. The words are grouped in several pairs, and then a trio: 'stones' and 'trees', 'move' and 'speak', 'Augures' and 'understood relations', and then three kinds of bird that can be taught to talk. Its verbs are of movement and speech, and conclude with an action of display: 'brought forth'. The single object follows this last verb at the start of a new line: 'The secret'st man of blood'. With this phrase the speech returns to 'blood', the repeated word of its first line, but now related through 'man' to Macbeth himself. It is at this point that, undoubtedly, Macbeth must look at his wife or in some way become conscious of her presence, for now he speaks to her. The question he asks is both simple and metaphorically resonant: 'What is the night?' It can hardly be that Macbeth needs to know the time for any immediate reason, for when he is answered he moves on to another, unrelated question: he may well ask the time because he looks at his wife, not the other way about.

The actors' responsibilities here are obvious. If Lady Macbeth has already moved towards her husband, his 'What is the night?' may be a response to her advance; and the following, 'How say'st thou, that Macduff denies his person At our great bidding?' could be an attempt to ask for help. If she has not moved at all and if he hardly looks at her for the first question, his words may sound like an attempted casualness, and the question about Macduff a pretence of sharing his thoughts with her to avoid further contact. Certainly after Lady Macbeth's direct question, 'Did you send to him sir?', he answers almost lightly, and then proceeds to speak only of himself. His information about spies could be spoken as much to reassure himself as to keep her attention or calm her doubts. The ambiguity is removed when he speaks decisively of his immediate actions, with a repeated 'I will' that shows an urgent need both for the assurance the witches can give and for belief in his own ability to act in this way.

The meeting between the two figures represented by the three questions is a dramatic event of great delicacy, the least change on either side being capable of altering the whole statement. Lady Macbeth's question, 'Did you send to him sir?', is so simple verbally that it can be spoken many ways; and yet it is crucial, for with these words she takes the 'lead' in the talk for the first time since she relinquished it on the departure of the guests. If she needs to know – awakened by the talk of 'blood' – why is it her only question? If it is an attempt to share his decisions, why is it her last? If it is intended to spur him to action, why is it phrased as a question in the past tense? Perhaps the question and form it takes are most acceptable as an almost automatic response that expects no answer, a means of establishing contact between man and wife. Or, possibly, it could be a sign that she has re-nounced her earlier decisive role; so she would speak with a new passivity, weakness and disorientation, a foretaste of her som-nambulance. The contrast with the rhythm and resonance of her previous speech may point towards such an interpretation of her question; perhaps she should now sit, and soon look away from her husband.

With Macbeth's decision to go to the witches, rhythms become stronger, breaking each line near its middle. But Macbeth's engagement is not constant for long, and at line 134 he introduces a note of explanation: 'for now I am bent to know . . .' This may be due to a renewed awareness of his wife's presence and interest, but, even if so, explanation soon gives way to self-assertion: 'for mine own good, All causes shall give way.' The specification of 'mine own good' could be interpreted as a rejection of Lady Macbeth's interests; certainly it leads to sustained self-awareness which, with a link backwards to the 'blood' of the first line, and a loss of future commitment, gives a still moment of feeling and immediate response: 'I am in blood . . .' Two verbs of physical action, 'Stepped' and 'wade', are introduced that are quite at variance with the simpler verbs that precede them in this duologue. A new tense is also introduced with 'should I wade no more', which is the only supposition in a run of affirmative verbs. The adjective 'tedious' also stands apart in this context, an almost domestic word, an understatement expressing deepest pain; it also has a positive statement of lengthening time, the realization of a continuing predicament in which weariness adds its weight to the already unendurable. Having drawn the episode forward with his decisiveness, Macbeth's mind seems to recoil upon himself until he is held by an acutely felt awareness of a timeless defilement, suffering and weakness.

During this part of his speech, metrical regularity is accentuated by the introduction of rhyming couplets. The first is somewhat hidden by the syntax, which leads on from the rhyming word to the following line, which has its own rhyme. But with 'Returning were as tedious as go o'er', metre, rhyme and syntax make a common end. This, probably, will be another point of rest, or rather of re-engagement. Lady Macbeth does not speak, but he seems to become conscious of her once more in that the following couplet is both explanation and an explicit claim to secrecy, a withholding of information. This must introduce a new kind of contact between the two figures, for she now speaks in reply. While he speaks to her, directly, about himself, although holding back from a full sharing of his thoughts, she speaks about him: it could be cruelly objective – and probably would sound so if she were still standing at her place of command – or it could express pity and concern. Because she speaks of '*all* natures' and because he, now, is probably seated in his 'borrowed robes', perhaps on the throne beside her, it might be an acknowledgement that both are stretched to the limit of endurance. His response, 'Come, we'll to sleep', shows that he has at least become conscious, for the first time in this episode, of their shared predicament: he uses her simple word 'sleep'; he introduces the first person plural, 'we'; he first calls her towards him with 'Come'. The fact that neither of them will sleep easily (made clear by their physical appearance and, possibly, by echoes of the 'Sleep no more' that Macbeth had earlier reiterated) suggests that an element of kind, mutual deception is implicit in their words. On this second, and probably fuller, meeting both lose, or pretend to lose, their awareness of the pressing actuality which now impels and imprisons them: physically, as stage spectacle, this meeting must be significantly different from the first; at least on his part, it is more aware of her needs and of his own.

After this second meeting which is basically static, the two figures must move off stage, together or separately. How they do this will reveal the next stage forward of the drama; and the longish distance they have to cross to leave the stage and the empty tables and stools they must negotiate, will make their physical movements extended in time and therefore capable of variation and development. One physical interpretation of the text is this:

> On hearing his agreement, Lady Macbeth moves towards the door; but he is held still by a returning sense of his own predicament – perhaps looking at her he is reminded of the basic isolation that has been accentuated since his secret initiative in the murder of Banquo.
>
> He speaks, at first echoing '*strange*' from his previous speech of explanation, but ending almost wholly in terms of personal resolve.

She is stopped near the door by his words, looks at him and meets his eyes; but she says nothing.

In response to her challenge, he claims common purpose with her; his words are part excuse and part plea for support:

We are yet but young in deed.

Such an interpretation depends on Lady Macbeth being in command and breaking the contact of their meeting first. She might well be the weaker and leave after him:

> With '*Come, we'll to sleep*', relieved to be in contact with his wife once more and so not alone in his terror, Macbeth moves towards the door. The explanation of his '*strange*' thoughts and '*strange*' actions at the banquet follows almost involuntarily as he goes, only hardening with awareness of the present predicament and need for action on the last words, '*wants hard use*'. At this point he again sees Lady Macbeth, still seated as she has been throughout the duologue, and his last sentence, '*We are yet but young in deed*', is spoken in pity for her, and as encouragement.

They meet in silence and go off together.

Or neither may move until the last word has been spoken:

> '*Come, we'll to sleep*' is followed by no move at all; both remain seated because the casual phrase, for all its suggestion of sympathy and purpose, cannot make either face the next move in their story, whatever that may be; the words were unrealistic. Macbeth quickly realizes that she will not lead him, so he takes the blame upon himself, still trying to undervalue their joint predicament, and at the end trying to summon energy for them both; the couplet ends, metaphorically, with an up-beat. Still neither moves until Macbeth explicitly and positively links his suffering with hers, paradoxically making pain the source of strength, or at least of impetus.

They rise together . . .

But then there is still a further choice: does he support her? or do they support each other? do they not touch at all? do they

follow each other's eyes, or do they look away? does he look
to the door, or does she? Any way of leaving the stage will give
opportunity for impressing deeply-felt and inarticulate reactions;
the characters are held for scrutiny, so that the audience views
the drama wholly in terms of their physical actions and interactions. The concluding words of the scene, with ambiguous
relevance and changing involvement for the speaker, show that
Shakespeare intended the end of this sensitive, far-ranging and
puzzling duologue to be sustained by the individually creative
enactment of the two actors.

The crucial line is the last, which follows the decisive couplet
and is either an unresolved half-line of verse or a speech that
eludes the metrical basis that has so firmly supported the rest
of the duologue. It can be spoken in many different ways; the
choice will depend precisely on the kind of contact that has been
achieved between the two actors in each particular performance.
Shakespeare has left it unfixed so that some part of it may always
be an improvisation, with the surprise, immediacy and inner
truth that can be fostered by such acting; it is the actor's means
of finding the exact crown for this highly dramatic scene of
supernatural or imaginary visitation, political disaster and personal
tragedy. In terms of denotive meaning there is little ambiguity:

> We (we two) – are (at this present, actual moment are) – yet
> (for the time being) – but (only, merely) – young (untried, at
> an early stage, weak, not yet full grown) – in deed (in doing and
> being; in moving from thoughts, strange, imperial or sensitive,
> to action, to deception, cunning, murder, to the task of forcing
> our imaginations into reality and our wills upon other men's).

The full force of these words, their meaning in terms of physically
realized human encounter, lies beyond all this, in the kind of
utterance they are given and the changing presence, movement,
tensions and relationship, of the two actors interpreting the roles.

Act V, Scene v

Enter, with drum and colours, MACBETH, SEYTON, *and* SOLDIERS

MACBETH: Hang out our banners on the outward walls.
The cry is still 'They come'. Our castle's strength
Will laugh a siege to scorn. Here let them lie
Till famine and the ague eat them up.
Were they not forced with those that should be ours,   5
We might have met them dareful, beard to beard,
And beat them backward home.   *A cry within, of women*
                              What is that noise?
SEYTON: It is the cry of women, my good lord.   [*Exit*]
MACBETH: I have almost forgot the taste of fears.
The time has been, my senses would have cooled   10
To hear a night-shriek, and my fell of hair
Would at a dismal treatise rouse and stir
As life were in't. I have supped full with horrors;
Direness, familiar to my slaughterous thoughts
Cannot once start me.

                    [*Enter* SEYTON]

                    Wherefore was that cry?   15
SEYTON: The Queen, my lord, is dead.
MACBETH: She should have died hereafter;
There would have been time for such a word.
Tomorrow, and tomorrow, and tomorrow,
Creeps in this petty pace from day to day,   20
To the last syllable of recorded time;
And all our yesterdays have lighted fools
The way to dusty death. Out, out, brief candle!
Life's but a walking shadow, a poor player,
That struts and frets his hour upon the stage,   25
And then is heard no more. It is a tale
Told by an idiot, full of sound and fury,
Signifying nothing.

                Enter a MESSENGER

Thou comest to use thy tongue. Thy story quickly.
MESSENGER: Gracious my lord,   30

I should report that which I say I saw,
But know not how to do't.
MACBETH: Well, say sir.
MESSENGER: As I did stand my watch upon the hill,
I looked toward Birnam, and anon methought
The wood began to move.
MACBETH: Liar and slave!   35
MESSENGER: Let me endure your wrath, if't be not so.
Within this three mile may you see it coming.
I say, a moving grove.
MACBETH: If thou speak'st false,
Upon the next tree shalt thou hang alive
Till famine cling thee. If thy speech be sooth,   40
I care not if thou dost for me as much.
I pull in resolution, and begin
To doubt th' equivocation of the fiend,
That lies like truth: 'Fear not, till Birnam wood
Do come to Dunsinane'; and now a wood   45
Comes toward Dunsinane. Arm, arm, and out!
If this which he avouches does appear,
There is nor flying hence, nor tarrying here.
I 'gin to be aweary of the sun,
And wish th' estate o' th' world were now undone.   50
Ring the alarum bell! Blow wind, come wrack,
At least we'll die with harness on our back.   *Exeunt*

This scene makes huge demands upon the actor of Macbeth. The
long episode in England, the murder of Lady Macduff and her
son, and Lady Macbeth's sleep-walking scene (IV. ii and iii and
V. i) have given him some respite, but already he has had one
scene of preparation for the final battle, full of sickness 'of heart'
(V. iii. 19), foreboding and defiance. Now the range of feeling
is still wider and the force of events and of his own conflicting
reactions has gained momentum, having more pressure and more
rapid movement.

    Within fifty-two lines the actor has to speak and embody senti-
ments as varied as these:

        Hang out our banners on the outward walls . . .

Here let them lie . . .

I have almost forgot the taste of fears . . .

She should have died hereafter . . .

And all our yesterdays have lighted fools
The way to dusty death.

Thou comest to use thy tongue. Thy story quickly.

Upon the next tree shalt thou hang alive
Till famine cling thee . . .

I pull in resolution, and begin
To doubt . . .

Arm, arm, and out!

I 'gin to be aweary of the sun . . .

Ring the alarum bell! Blow wind, come wrack . . .

The contradictions in purpose are plain enough: Macbeth must change from defence to attack, from 'Here let them lie' to 'Arm, arm, and out!' He must seem beyond fear, and then gripped by doubt and angry with apprehension. At first he believes time to be on his side, and then devalues all past time; he later demands a story 'quickly', and finally is oppressed by the very thought of continuing time. His attitude to death is at first callous, then pathetic, and then desperate and scornful; later he welcomes death for himself and for the whole world; and at last he draws death, defiantly, upon himself.

There are two main problems for the actor, supposing that he has the necessary imagination, strength and technique to create each verbal statement so that it is true both in itself and in relationship to physical performance. Firstly, he must be able to make the transitions from one involvement to another so that the contrasts are clear and the process believable, or at least acceptable, to himself and to his audience. Secondly, he must find a sustaining 'through line',[1] or psychological and physical unity, for the scene as a whole and in relation to the whole play.

Four of the major transitions are activated by agencies that

[1] See pages 32-3, above.

are clearly outside Macbeth himself. The first two are linked: a
'*cry . . . of women*' and then Seyton's bare, factual statement.
Macbeth has been scornfully assured, seeing his enemies, including
those 'that should be ours', as food for famine and fever to devour;
the use of 'forced', for 'reinforced' carries a pun on '*farcé*' or
'stuffed'. But he does not stay with these thoughts; he moves on
towards an imagined conflict where he could be active and 'dareful' – this word is an invention, the *Oxford English Dictionary*
quoting only this passage and a subsequent poetic description. He
conceives of the closest contact, 'beard to beard', and a physical
and final victory against sustained resistance: 'and beat them backward home'. This is all what 'might have' been, and so the actual
cry of women, even though heard from a distance, immediately
catches his attention. The women's voices, following the word
'home', could well seem appropriate to his imaginary conflict,
but there is no colour in his words: for him, the cry is simply
'that noise'. Among cries of horror there must be a cry of pain,
for his wife is dying by 'self and violent hands' (V. ix. 35); but
Macbeth does not betray, in his choice of words, whether he
recognizes the voice in torment or not. Then Seyton replies, and
his noncommittal word 'women' must bring a closer understanding for Macbeth; the loyal servant's '*good* lord' may suggest a
careful delivery, aware of all the implications. Another transition
for Macbeth is now inevitable; he can no longer be, or pretend
to be, efficient and soldierly.

So far the two main kinds of transition have already been shown
in this scene: the changes that develop because of the restlessness
in Macbeth's own mind – as when he seems drawn from scorn
to imagined bravery – and those which are forced on him by the
situation as it develops around him. This is not to say that Macbeth is active and then passive, for with the latter kind of transition
Shakespeare introduces surprise so that his mind seems to move,
even here, by his own volition as well as outward necessity. After
Seyton's reply, Macbeth has one sentence that is a complete
and almost regular verse-line and, surprisingly, it expresses self-
awareness rather than a response to the immediate possibilities of

the situation. It follows the full emotional response rather than carries it, for the verb is in the perfect tense:

> I have almost forgot the taste of fears.

The 'almost' and 'taste' show that he *has* experienced fear following the women's cries; but this does not preclude other responses as well, that could more directly motivate him towards this descriptive self-awareness. His words continue to describe fearful occurrences, but emphasize his own sensual and physical responses; and on 'supped full', he suggests that he has actively participated in past horrors. On this cue, with 'Direness' and 'slaughterous', two words that are found only here in Shakespeare's works, he moves to the present tense; what he now acknowledges is that, in his response to the cries, 'Direness' had found an echo in his own murderous intentions. This word was invented by Shakespeare from 'dire', which had only recently, in 1567, been adopted into English from the Latin *dirus*, meaning 'portentous' as much as 'fearful'. After the surprise of Macbeth's apparent dismissal of 'fears', his words show that he continues to be held by fear and fatefulness, as well as maintaining self-awareness. He also moves from description to renewed assertion, as if seeking instinctively for courage or defiance.

The next transition is forced by Seyton's silent re-entry. Macbeth turns to him at once to question the reason for 'that cry' – it is no longer simply that 'noise'. Two half-lines show that silence is an integral part of the drama at this moment, but where the pauses come is not clear. Seyton may well take time before he speaks, or during his three-phrased sentence, 'The Queen, my lord, is dead.' Macbeth must create a silence before or after 'She should have died hereafter'; the fact that his next line is closely linked with this, the break usually being represented by a semi-colon or comma, rather than a full-stop, suggests that the main pause is before he has spoken at all. So, as in the previous reaction to Seyton's words, Macbeth speaks after the first response has been made in silence; only this time the thought which he does utter is directly concerned with his wife and with what might

have been, and not with his own experience. This much is clear
by contrast with his earlier response, but the exact meaning of his
words is notoriously difficult to fix. Shakespeare has made him
speak a kind of riddle. Perhaps there is a wry, self-critical humour
intended as a pitiful defence against too-precise thought, which
might explain the following 'There would have been a time for
such a word.' Perhaps 'should have died' carries the common
Elizabethan sense of 'inevitably would have died', for this
would link with Macbeth's awareness of fate immediately before.
Perhaps the defiance in his earlier 'Cannot once start me' argues
that he is now rebuking Fate, for all the absurd ineffectualness of
such a reaction. If Shakespeare had wanted Macbeth to react with
perfect clarity there is little reason to suppose that he could
not have provided an unambiguous response: as the text stands,
Macbeth seems stunned by the news and his words most eloquent
as an attempt to become aware of what has happened to his wife,
to himself, and to his whole world. The subtextual strength of the
passage is Macbeth's desire to be in control and to find an appropriate action; its effect is of inner struggle and then compromise.

After the riddle, there is a slower development. Macbeth's
words seem to be spoken to no one, and possibly a full command of
his own consciousness does not come immediately. At first he
plays with another riddle, man's awareness of Yesterday–Today–
Tomorrow: the inevitable daily change that leaves tomorrow
always the spur to effort and yesterday the reminder of futility,
and all time recorded as if it were a fateful process towards a
finality, the last syllable of which will lack a meaning in itself.
His self-awareness has now returned, but in the widest possible
terms. With quickening rhythm and a histrionic apostrophe, he
moves once more to the present time with a call for death which
invokes biblical imagery of life as a 'candle'. Freed from precise
concern with his wife or himself, his mind is now moving quickly;
this image lasts for a moment only and other biblical images
follow: life as a 'tale' that is told, and as an 'ignorant' and 'vain'
shadow walking upon earth.[1] With this general invocation of

---

[1] See *Psalms* 17: 28, 39: 7 and 90: 9; *Job* 8: 9 and 18: 6; *Proverbs* 20: 27.

death and contempt of life, Macbeth introduces three human images, three man-centred concepts. The first is general, of mankind as 'fools'. The second particularizes a 'poor player', who 'struts and frets' upon a stage as any insufficient actor might do if he tried for immediate effect rather than the creation of the man he was intended to impersonate:[1] and the player is one who is given no second opportunity to perform. The third human image is still more complicated, for life is no longer envisaged in palpable human actions, but as having the reality only of a tale as it is being told; the human figure is the speaker, and he is an 'idiot'. In this last vision, men are pawns or puppets activated by an incomprehending and mad creator: there is 'sound and fury' in the tale, but this implies no meaning and no significant conclusion. Despair has brought Macbeth to a loss of conviction and of a sense of identity; only his speaking voice and presence on stage affirm his continued existence, for his words deny any manageable reality. 'Signifying nothing' is a half-line, so the last expression of Macbeth following Seyton's news may well be silence; and this silence would not cover an instinctive movement towards self-awareness and control.

At this static moment, the last of the interruptions occurs: the entry of a frightened, speechless, almost 'idiot' messenger, a man who has to tell an impossible tale. Macbeth alters at once, for his despair is challenged: impatiently he takes command until the news is out and he hears the words of the witches' prophecy. Again he changes rapidly: to a 'wrath' that expresses his wish to disbelieve; to a defensive threat of slow death; to a renewed self-awareness. There is an obvious dramatic irony in Macbeth's need to know the messenger's story when he has just dismissed life itself as a meaningless 'tale'. The immediate energy of his responses and his temporary lack of self-awareness are also strongly contrasted with the preceding speeches that had followed a silent reaction to news. He moves with unreflecting speed, only to be caught by an antithesis, like others in the play, between 'good'

[1] It is notable that Shakespeare in two other places associates a bad actor with 'strutting'; see *Hamlet*, III. ii. 36, and *Troilus and Cressida*, I. iii. 153.

and 'ill', 'fair' and 'foul': from his angry 'If thou speak'st false' (38) his mind leaps to the opposite, 'If thy speech be sooth . . .' (40). Then the messenger is almost forgotten, and soon will be entirely, in self-awareness. Certainty, or 'resolution', is now drawn back,[1] and as he remembers himself he also precisely remembers the witches' words as 'equivocation', a mixture of lies and truth.

The words 'and now a wood Comes toward Dunsinane' (45–6) bring Macbeth back to a sense of the present moment, and instinctively he again loses all his self-awareness in a cry for attack. He speaks now with the support of rhyme and his words start the line of reaction that will carry him off stage at the concluding couplet, with the bell ringing as it had done for the death of Duncan (see II. i. 62). He can now defy storm and disaster in the thought that he will fight, that he has positive action to perform. There is, of course, an irony in the image he uses, that sees armour as a load-bearing 'harness' in which he can be directed; so it is clear that he sees himself dying in battle because of the working-out of his fate as well as because of his instinctive decision. There is pride, too, in the concluding couplet, unmistakably present for the first time in this scene: in the deprecating 'At least', the use of the royal plural, and the contrasts with the 'If . . .' and falling rhythms that followed the first 'Arm, arm, and out!'

Between these two commands to fight, there is, however, another couplet, representing two more momentous transitions of mood: a movement to a quiet and still awareness like that following the death of the Queen, and then a movement back into action once more. Macbeth's consciousness of futility has significantly developed: he now speaks directly of himself, and, in 'I 'gin', with a sense that he is still descending towards a full experience of life-weariness; instead of 'life', he talks about the 'sun', the life-giving power marking the progress of each day. But if all this shows an access of personal consciousness, it is balanced in the second line of the couplet with a wish that the

[1] Some editors emend to 'pall', meaning 'fail'; but the physical activity of reining in may not be inappropriate to Macbeth's view of himself, even if he does, in fact, let certainty go when it has already deserted him.

whole basis of human life and society were 'undone' with him, and that this was 'now', without the further defiance to which some pressure within his being forces him. Macbeth is torn between acceptance of defeat and defiant activity, and the pain he suffers comes as much from these tensions within him as from his obvious physical weariness and isolation.

As he leaves the stage, Macbeth is, for the time being, in command. This human image is the more compelling for contrast with the following muffled, and almost inhuman, entry of Malcolm and his army carrying green boughs. For the moment Macbeth will dominate, but Malcolm directs that the 'leafy screens' (V. vi. 1) be thrown down, and the stage is filled with soldiers, an image of new life, of fulfilment of the witches' prophecy and of outnumbering and well-ordered power.

This contrast may provide one guide to the 'through-line' for the scene as a whole. Presumably Macbeth's first order, 'Hang out our banners . . .' (1), had sent almost all his followers off-stage. Certainly the main business of the scene will best be staged with Macbeth alone except for Seyton and, later, the messenger. Soldiers may well return as he gives the order to arm, but they will only accentuate his new isolation, for the change of tactics will be wholly unexpected by them, and the energy be Macbeth's alone. If some soldiers have remained on stage throughout the scene, the variety and power of Macbeth's responses, contrasted with their silent incomprehension, would mark him as a man apart. At the end of the scene the visual image makes a direct statement: Macbeth, alone and with 'harness' on his back, defying his enemies and life itself as he has come to know it.

In this scene, then, Macbeth becomes himself, alone and appallingly whole. Later events will press more strongly upon him, but here he has also responded in his own time; he has confronted idiocy and silence as well as the instinctive need for decision and courage. In this sense it is a trumph: Macbeth has murdered and has committed great outrages, and now his imagination has no use for the sun and wishes the 'estate o' th' world' undone, but he has not killed his own will to be himself. He discovers and uses the last resources of his being, even if this destroys affection, sensitivity, intelligence and desire, and even if these responses die, as they are seen to do in this scene, slowly and painfully. Macbeth does not speak of his determination to 'try the last' until just before his last fight (V. viii. 32), and no one else draws attention to it, but his struggle in this scene – its wide range and variety of mood, and the fierceness of its transitions – shows that deep within him is a lust for purity, a self-centred, intolerant, reckless and sustained drive towards a realization of himself that is both whole and intense. By following this lust, he is left, at last, caught: alone, hopeless, committed to the reality of his imaginative world in which an idea of himself had burned with an intensity sufficient to destroy himself and many other lives with him.

As it works out its course, this lust burns a greatly gifted man to destruction, illuminating the qualities that are its source and fuel. For example, the verbal images in this scene show that, for Macbeth, life has pride, splendour and strength of physical response:

> Our castle's *strength*
> Will *laugh* a siege to *scorn*.   (2–3)

Death is a devouring and withering alternative to life, ready with appropriate action:

> Upon the next tree shalt thou hang alive
> Till famine cling thee.   (39–40)

Time is deft and active – with 'petty pace' (20) – and gives necessary light – there is both the 'candle' and the 'sun' (23 and 49) – to fools and to soldiers. When Macbeth thinks of defeat, his words are still essentially active – 'flying' and 'tarrying' – and closely linked together. In anger, he cries 'Liar and slave!' (35): the first word is a direct counterstatement, pinning the blame upon the man himself, and 'slave' speaks for Macbeth's scorn of men who cannot command themselves. When he talks to others, his orders are direct: 'Hang out our banners . . . What is that

noise?...Wherefore was that cry?...Thy story quickly...
Well, say sir.... Arm, arm, and out!... Ring the alarum bell!'
He apostrophizes life and destruction in the same manner: 'Out,
out, brief candle!...Blow wind, come wrack...' In personal
feeling, for his wife and for the failure of his own life and society,
he has no immediate words at all, rather an opposing silence of
acceptance and of pain. Only when he is once more in command
and committed to action does he speak of his deepest loss directly;
and then he uses words of apocalyptic grandeur:

> I 'gin to be aweary of the sun,
> And wish th' estate o' th' world were now undone. (49-50)

Nowhere in the play is judgement passed on Macbeth by a man
who knows how he has lived. The results of his death in political
terms are perfectly clear – 'The time is free!' (V. ix. 21) – and
so are the more personal afflictions caused by this 'dead butcher'
(V. ix. 35). The only account of Macbeth's state of mind comes,
by report, before the last battle:

> Some say he's mad; others, that lesser hate him,
> Do call it valiant fury . . .
>
> . . . Who then shall blame
> His pestered senses to recoil, and start,
> When all that is within him does condemn
> Itself for being there?   (V. ii. 12-25)

What is missing in this account is the sustained self-realization,
largeness of mind, fineness of feeling: the clarity, silences, and
sober strength; the knowledge of his isolation and inescapable
annihilation. Names like 'worthy thane', 'peerless kinsman',
'Great Glamis', are forgotten in the dialogue of the end of the
play.

Shakespeare poses none of the obvious questions: if Macbeth
had not been isolated, would he have destroyed? if he were not
greatly gifted in mind and body, would he have been isolated?
if he had no imaginative life, seeing himself as a king among
men, would he have murdered? if he had not sought courage,

would his wife have persuaded him? if he had not required a 'settled' wholeness to his life (I. vii. 79–80), would he have been remarkable? While Shakespeare does not make any comment, his dramatic style draws precise attention to all these sources of Macbeth's life, and their interplay provides many of the emotional, physical and verbal crises of the action. Macbeth is progressively revealed so that the audience is caught up in his deepest thoughts and most instinctive reactions, at the same time as it is made increasingly aware of the great evils that result from his life.